# Praise f
## *The Writing Irish of New York*

This collection of essays and remembrances is bursting at the seams with talent. Irish writers finding their voice in New York City is a long and revered tradition, and this book shows that tradition to be alive and well in the new century. If it's wit, wisdom and dazzling prose that you're looking for, *The Writing Irish of New York* will not disappoint.

**T.J. English**, *New York Times* bestselling author of *The Savage City*

This is a fascinating book which I read at one sitting—containing no end of insight, with chunks of unanticipated wisdom and the finest of contemporary writing. A delicious feast.

**Patrick McCabe**, author of *The Butcher Boy* and *Breakfast on Pluto*

This carefully curated collection of essays represents both the old guard and young guns on the New York literary scene, and feels like a true representation of the New York Irish experience. Almost all of these well written and insightful essays illustrate what's it feels like to be Irish-American as opposed to Irish-in-America.

**Kate Kerrigan**, *New York Times* bestselling author of *The Dress*

Here are extraordinary and vivid essays by and about many of the people who first spring to mind when you think of Irish writers and New York City: Frank McCourt and Brendan Behan, Maeve Brennan and Scott Fitzgerald, Eugene O'Neill and Jimmy Breslin. But the book's true delight, and it's revelation, are the surprising voices you may not have heard before: Malachy, the other McCourt brother, and his ball-breaking humor; Larry Kirwan, the bard of Black 47; Maura Mulligan, a dancer and a deeply authentic witness to the joy of discovering a creative life; Brian O'Sullivan, an off-the-boat plasterer by trade who happens to write with a Twain-like appreciation for the absurd truths of life; and Kevin Fortuna, a spellbinding storyteller with a newfound deep connection to the old country. There are many others, and their indelible portraits stick with you, and what you thought you knew about a people and a place becomes ever so much richer.

**John Kenney**, Managing Editor, *Esquire*

# The Writing Irish of New York

*Edited by*

## Colin Broderick

Lavender Ink
lavenderink.org

*The Writing Irish of New York*
Colin Broderick, ed.

Copyright © 2018 by the author and Lavender Ink,
an imprint of Diálogos Books.

Printed in the U.S.A.
First Printing
10 9 8 7 6 5 4 3 2 1    18 19 20 21 22 23

Book design: Bill Lavender
Front cover design by Daria Milas
Author photo by Wojtek Urbanek

Library of Congress Control Number: 2018947210
Broderick, Colin
*The Writing Irish of New York* / Colin Broderick;
p. cm.
ISBN: 978-1-944884-53-6 (cloth)
978-1-944884-51-2 (pbk.)
978-1-944884-52-9 (ebook)

# Lavender Ink
lavenderink.org

# Photo Credits

All photos by Colin Broderick unless otherwise noted here.

Maeve Brennan (29): Nina Leen/The LIFE Picture Collection/Getty Images.

Frank McCourt (42): by Elke Wetzig (Creative Commons).

Jimmy Breslin (87): at the 2008 Brooklyn Book Festival, by David Shankbone (Creative Commons).

JP Donleavy with Brendan Behan, and Philip Wiseman (139): 1959, *Daily Mail*/Rex/Shutterstock (Fair Use).

Billy Collins (167): by Bill Hayes.

Frank O'Hara (169): 1965, by Mario Schifano (Fair Use).

John F. Kennedy Jr. (178): NASA photo (Public Domain).

Colum McCann (181): by Christian McCann.

Brendan Behan (199): *New York World-Telegram and the Sun,* staff photograph by Walter Albertin (Library of Congress).

Oscar Wilde (233): Metropolitan Museum of Art, by Napoleon Sarony (Creative Commons).

# The Writing Irish of New York

This book is dedicated to
Rachel
my divine light.

And to my children
Erica, and Samuel
who remain my greatest teachers.

# The Writing Irish
# of New York

# Who Are the Writing Irish of New York?

Perhaps what I am trying to do with this book is exactly what I've been trying to do with everything else I write. I'm trying to figure out who I am and what my place in the world is.

Identity is a funny thing. We are always looking for ways to identify ourselves. We identify ourselves by sex, skin color, language, country of origin. We do it almost without thinking. It's how we're wired. We cling to identity because the story we create about ourselves solidifies the notion of who we believe we are in the world. And that story gives us comfort.

It certainly gives me comfort to think I know who I am, and the act of writing has always helped me wipe the mirror clean so I can say, "Ah, there you are."

So who am I?

I am Irish. I live in New York. I am a writer. I am an Irish writer in New York. But what does that mean?

Let me start with the Irish part. I come from Northern Ireland, which some refer to as the United Kingdom. But I've never wanted to be a part of a kingdom. I prefer to think of myself as a free agent. There's something in my Irish nature that seems to be opposed to kings and queens and oppression in all its forms, something in fact that doesn't like to be dominated at all.

So I say: "I'm Irish." Although I was actually born in England. Stratford Road, Birmingham, to be precise. But I was only there for two months as an infant before my parents moved my older brother, Michael, and me back home to County Tyrone, where we were raised. Does that make me English? No. I am Irish because I say it is so.

I am Irish because I can construct a believable story around my Irishness.

I have lived in New York for the last twenty-nine years—

much longer than I actually lived in Ireland—but I still say I'm Irish, although perhaps I am Irish-American now. Wouldn't that make sense too?

When I first arrived in America, I was living in the Bronx. I was an angry drunk young carpenter, and I hated the term "Irish-American." How dare anyone who did not have an Irish accent say they were Irish! It's ridiculous, right?

It took me a long time to shed my ignorance, to embrace the Irish diaspora, not just here in America but in Australia and England and everywhere else we drifted after hunger sent us fluttering like sycamore seeds in the fall.

I am a writer. But I am also a carpenter and a housepainter and a floor sander. So why don't I just stick with one of those other noble trades as a way of identifying myself in the world? Why?

It's because I have finally come to understand and accept my relationship to writing. It's a relationship that has more to do with my thinking than with my writing. I cannot escape the way my thinking demands writing of me. Writing has been an inherent part of who I am in the world since my earliest memories.

So who am I, in this context? I am an Irish writer in New York. I am an Irish voice in a long line of Irish voices who have wrestled, pen in hand, with these exact same issues of identity and exile for the past 150 years or so, here, in America.

The more I read into my past, into our past as Irish-Americans, the more I see that all our stories are stitched together with a fine green thread.

It's a very recent phenomenon, this idea of a writing Irish identity in New York, certainly in terms of any sort of community. The first book of Irish-American fiction was published in Winchester, Virginia, in 1877 by a Hibernian named Adam Douglas. It was, like most other Irish writing at the time, highly nationalistic in theme.

New York itself is a relative newcomer as a city. So if you take a glance back at the history of Irish writing here in this town, nothing much of note really occurs until after the famine years.

By 1860, one in every four New Yorkers was Irish. But even then, the Irish literary voice in New York could be heard only in journalistic fragments, or nationalist publications like John Devoy's *Irish Nation,* or religious or historical novels by the likes of Mary Anne Sadlier, a writer whose career benefited greatly, it seems, from the fact that her husband owned a major publishing house.

There were other Irish American novels at the time, but history would prove them in large part forgettable. They were stories steeped in nostalgia, sentimentalism, gentility, romanticism. It's important to consider the voice in terms of what was permissible by the church at the time. In short, it was a lot of writing without very much character at all, a lot of writing that's hard to get excited about.

Things didn't really start getting exciting—and by exciting I do mean sexy—until James Joyce's *Ulysses* got dragged into court here in the United States in 1920 for its references to masturbation. That was the same year Eugene O'Neill won the Pulitzer Prize for his first full-length play, *Beyond the Horizon.* Irish writing in New York had taken a profound and sudden turn. Pitch onto that smoldering pile of pages a New York novel called *The Great Gatsby* by a young Irish-American author named Francis Scott Fitzgerald and the whole thing suddenly ignited. The notion of an Irish-American literary identity had been born.

Into this sexy, post-famine, post-nationalist, post-propaganda era in Irish-American letters were delivered the likes of William Kennedy, Brian Friel, Pete Hamill, J. P. Dunleavy, Frank and Malachy McCourt. Toss in Brendan Behan and Maeve Brennan up through the 1950's and 1960's and it becomes apparent that what we are witnessing is the emergence of a new breed of writers and thinkers: the advent of the Irish Writer in America as Mythical Figure. It was a new and exciting identity, an identity a young adventurous boy, or girl, might well aspire to.

By the eighties and nineties a community was emerging, a community with a cultural identity, with a fresh band of authors steering the way: Colum McCann, T. J. English, Edna O'Brien, Peter Quinn, Mary Pat Kelly, John Patrick Shanley, and too many other wonderful writers to mention here, a community that didn't really coalesce, I would argue, until the formation of the Irish American Writers and Artists Association in 2008.

This book is an attempt to capture the essence of what that writing community feels like as a whole.

We live in a precarious time for authors. The publishing world, as with all forms of media, has become concerned more with celebrity than with content. Contemporary Irish authors whose talent may have afforded them a modest living just thirty years ago are now forced to work two or three jobs just to keep a roof over their heads. New York has become a city almost impossible to survive in as an artist. It is a city of tourists and finance wizards. And yet a handful of Irish writers continue to persevere here. They dodge and weave, spin and hustle—anything to make a buck to keep the pen moving along. If you look carefully, you will see them, stepping along amid the skyscrapers, a little disheveled perhaps, their gaze inward as they plot their next move. They are a community worth honoring, for they are on the front lines, fighting to keep the tradition alive. They are the shamans, fighting against all odds to keep reminding us, as a tribe, who we are. They are a vital conduit to our collective identity.

This collection is my sincere attempt to portray what that community looks like today. Many of these Irish writers you will never have heard of; others have reached the pinnacle of Irish-American letters. But in the overall fabric of the writing Irish community, each voice is invaluable.

There is a fine green thread that binds us all.
We are the Writing Irish of New York.

Colin Broderick

# Peter Quinn

Peter Quinn is the author of *Hour of the Cat, The Man Who Never Returned, Looking for Jimmy, Dry Bones,* and *The Banished Children of Eve.* He has worked as a speechwriter for New York governors Hugh Carey and Mario Cuomo, and as the editorial director for Time Warner. He is a third-generation New Yorker whose grandparents were born in Ireland.

# Recollections of a B.I.C.

Breathes there the man, with soul so dead,
Who never to himself hath said,
This is my own, my native land!
Whose heart hath ne'er within him burn'd,
As home his footsteps he hath turn'd..."

*—Sir Walter Scott*

"Native land" means different things to different people. To some it's a nation with well-defined borders, like France or Sweden; to others, it transcends borders, à la Ireland or Korea. For many, I think, native land invokes something more intimate and parochial: a patch of earth that, no matter where life takes us, stays synonymous with home. For me, that place is the Bronx of the 1950s and 60s, a lower-middle/middle-middle-class agglomeration of apartment houses, single-family homes, and small businesses sprawled between Long Island Sound to the east and the Hudson River to the west, a so-called bedroom borough whose north-south subway lines transported its inhabitants to and from jobs in Manhattan.

Reeking of exhaust and incinerators, the Bronx was chockablock with pizzerias, German and Jewish delis, Irish bars; blessed with spacious parks, a world-class zoo and botanical garden; and possessed of the Ruthian diamond—the crown jewel of major league baseball—Yankee Stadium. The skyline looming to the south was the imperial city, a dream-big place, proximate yet far away. Ours was the workaday, no-illusion city, its concrete precincts filled with cops, firemen, pipefitters, clerks, mechanics, motormen, taxi drivers, teachers, housewives, shop owners, wire lathers, civil servants, and union members, the everyday people who kept the place running.

Solid, stolid, often the butt of jokes ("The Bronx, no thonx" wrote Ogden Nash), the borough was a small-scale Yugoslavia: ethnic enclaves interspersed with areas in which, though physically mingled, groups lived psychically and culturally apart. Jews, by far the most numerous population, branched out from the Art Deco stem of the Grand Course. Highbridge, Kingsbridge, and Woodlawn were heavily Irish. Fordham, presided over by the Jesuit Gothic of the eponymous university, was bordered to the west by the well-heeled Irish parish of St. Nicholas of Tolentine; to the southeast by Belmont, a tight-knit Italian village of modest apartment buildings and meticulously tended one- and two-family homes.

The once Irish/Jewish South Bronx filled with newly arrived Puerto Ricans and African Americans. The East Bronx was a trifecta of Jews, Irish, and Italians. Riverdale, in the borough's northwest corner, felt like an appendage of suburban Westchester County. Fieldston, adjacent to it, was a privately owned enclave of privilege and palatial homes.

Home to almost a million-and-a half people, the borough had only one real hotel, the Concourse Plaza. It was often referred to as the "Bronx's Waldorf Astoria," a description more aspirational than exact, which is not to say it wasn't a fine place to spend the night. Around the corner from where my wife was raised and a Mickey Mantle home run away from Yankee Stadium, the Concourse Plaza is at the center of the 1956 movie, *A Catered Affair*, a tale of working-class Irish-Catholic parents in conflict over their daughter's wedding reception.

In an improbable feat of casting, the taxi-driving, Irish-Catholic dad is played by Ernest Borgnine, the daughter by Debbie Reynolds, and the mother by Bette Davis, whose attempt at a Bronx accent is somewhere between a misfire and weird. (Barry Fitzgerald, her brother, has a rich Irish brogue, a discrepancy left unexplained.) The movie was based on a television play by Bronx-native Paddy Chayefsky, who the previous year had won the Academy Award for best screenplay for *Marty*, another Bronx tale with Ernest Borgnine in his Academy Award-winning role as an Italian-American butcher.

I recall *Marty* receiving accolades from relatives and neighbors. Scenes shot in the Bronx and mention of places like Fordham Road and Arthur Avenue sprinkled Hollywood stardust over the borough's prosaic precincts. As opposed to *Marty*, which had a ring of authenticity, *A Catered Affair* was a blatant attempt to piggyback off the success of its predecessor, with Irish characters substituted for Italian. The screenplay was written by Gore Vidal who, if pressed, could probably have located the Bronx somewhere between Montreal and the Upper East Side. The movie earned mostly Bronx cheers.

We Bronx Irish defined ourselves as much by parishes as neighborhoods. I was from St. Raymond's, in Parkchester, in the East Bronx. Founded in 1842, it was the first Catholic church in Westchester County. (The Bronx became a separate county in 1914. The five boroughs of New York City are coterminous with state counties.) In the burial yard in front of the church were three towering Celtic crosses, monuments to the half-century reign of a triad of Irish monsignori. Despite all belonging to the genus of B.I.C. (Bronx Irish Catholic), we at St. Raymond Elementary School considered ourselves distinctly different from our counterparts in the cheek-by-jowl parish of St. Helena's.

A planned community of 12,000 apartments spread across 171 buildings of 7-13 stories, Parkchester was created by the Metropolitan Life Insurance Company, which also financed construction of Stuyvesant Town in Manhattan. Parks and open spaces were strategically placed. The main means of transportation were subways and the extensive system of city-owned bus lines. But in prescient anticipation of a rapid increase in car ownership, there were multistoried garages and copious parking spaces.

Parkchester's residents were overwhelmingly Jewish and Catholics (Irish in the main). The few Protestants were regarded with curiosity. Up until the 1960s, Metropolitan Life excluded African Americans from both Stuyvesant Town and Parkchester. This was of a piece with the intransigent residential segregation that prevailed (and still prevails) across large swathes of the city. Desperate to increase the supply of middle-class housing—at least for whites—New York's progressive mayor, Fiorello LaGuardia, reluctantly went along. (Ironically, the oval at Parkchester's center once contained the ballfield on which the Negro League's Lincoln Giants played their home games.)

Parkchester was built on the site of the old Catholic Protectory, which was founded in 1863 by Archbishop John Hughes, the Ulster-born hierarch who established Fordham University, initiated the building of St. Patrick's cathedral, and made the New York Irish into a political as well as religious constituency. The Protectory housed orphans and abandoned children, mostly Irish, whom the Children's Aid Society had begun shipping west on "Orphan Trains" to be settled among God-fearing, Anglo-Saxon Protestants.

Bordering Parkchester, Morris Park to the west and Castle Hill to the east were heavily Italian. A step behind in terms of assimilation and economic advancement, Italians generally preferred houses with small gardens over apartments. Parochial schools brought us together. Friendships blossomed and so did fights. I remember the schoolyard of St. Raymond's as an asphalt Serengeti where the weak were bullied and Irish toughs battled tough Italians. (Pugilistically inept, I did my best to be inconspicuous.)

Sometimes the rivalries were humorous. One Italian carting company emblazoned on its garbage trucks "We Cater Irish

Weddings." When I heard talk of "intermarriage" it referred to Irish-Italian nuptials. It wasn't until later that miscegenation escalated into ethnic meltdown and bred a new strain of Hiberno-Mediterranean offspring notable for their good looks.

Over the years, I've heard from Jewish Bronxites about suffering verbal harassment ("kikes," "sheenies," "Christ-killers") and physical abuse from, as one friend put it, "Irish pogromists." Without doubting their accounts, that wasn't my experience. Through all my years of parochial school, I never heard anti-Semitic professions by teachers or clergy. We were told it was our sins that nailed Jesus to the cross. If either of my parents suspected we were cursing or bullying Jews, retribution would have been swift and severe. Yet I had no Jewish friends. We lived separately together. One thing shared by gentiles and Jews was a familiarity with Yiddish. To be a Bronxite was to schlepp and kibitz, and to understand the difference between a smuck and a mensch.

I had no acquaintance with Jewish girls, except one. We rode the 20 BX bus together, she to Walton Girls High School in Kingsbridge, me to all-male Manhattan Prep in Riverdale. I sat in the back with my school buddies, she in front with her classmates. The first time I saw her, I was smitten by her thin and graceful figure, clothes loose and flowing (our style then was tight), thick, black curls (the fashion was long and straight), an early blossoming flower child. It was part of growing up in the Bronx to figure out, as quickly as possible, a person's tribe. I identified her Jewishness in the same way, if she bothered to notice, she perceived my goyishness.

We never spoke. And then, one September, she was gone, off to college I presumed. I spent months bereft. Recently, for the first time in fifty years, I rode a bus along the old route, and it all flooded back, my lonely-hearts Bronx tale, unbridgeable worlds in the same borough, on the same bus.

My first ancestors arrived in New York when Margaret and Michael Manning fled the Great Famine. Margaret Manning, their daughter and my paternal grandmother, was born in 1867, in the village of Fordham, at that time part of Westchester County. My grandfather Patrick Quinn, a union organizer, was born in Tipperary in 1859. His family emigrated to New York in 1870. He married Margaret Manning, a seamstress, in St. Brigid's church, on the Lower East Side, in 1899. They moved to the Bronx in 1914, where they bought a small house in the West Farms neighborhood which, despite its name, was absent all things agricultural.

Contra the notion of Irish obsession with ancestry, my family showed little interest in the past. My mother had an active disinterest, routinely tossing out documents and obfuscating or bowdlerizing the fate of relatives who fell victim to impoverishment or their own misbehaviors (or both). The primary focus of my parents and grandparents wasn't on the Irish past but the American future, and their children's role in it.

My father recalled that as a boy on the Lower East Side he shared a room with his older brother in which they rarely stayed. My grandparents hosted relative after relative as they arrived from Ireland, until none were left to bring over. If my grandfather heard anyone sentimentalizing about the old country his instant riposte was, "If you miss it so much, why don't you go back?" Romantic Ireland didn't ring very convincingly in crowded tenement rooms.

Catherine Riordan of Blarney, County Cork, landed at Castle Garden in 1888. (It would be four years before Ellis Island opened and processed its first immigrant, Annie Moore, also of County Cork.) Though Catherine claimed to be eighteen, it's more likely she was fifteen or sixteen and lied about her age so she could join her older sister as a domestic and begin sending remittances home to finance her siblings' journeys. She stayed at maid's work until she met James Murphy, a native-Irish speaker from near Macroom, who worked as a mechanic at Yorkville's Rupert Brewery. My mother, Viola Murphy, the last of their six children, was born on the top floor of a four-story walkup on 149th Street, in the Bronx.

Coming of age in the1920s, my parents belonged to the first truly modern generation. Electricity rolled back night and blazed the Great White Way. New appliances alleviated the burden of ancient drudgeries. Movies and radio revolutionized entertainment. Cars and airplanes shrank old barriers of distance. Credit and the installment plan made commonplace what were once luxuries. People's expectations rose exponentially. The population of the Bronx tripled to 1.2 million in 1930 from 400,000 in 1910. Progress and prosperity were presumed, with America in the vanguard, and Jazz Age New York ahead of all.

Where none of my grandparents went beyond primary school, my parents graduated college. My father received a B.S. in civil engineering from Manhattan College (despite its name, it's in the Bronx) and worked on the construction of the IND subway while attending Fordham Law School at night. My mother was a classics major at Mt. Saint Vincent, in Riverdale. They met in 1928 at a parish St. Patrick's Day dance in the Bronx. They loved nightclubs, the theater—musicals, the Marx Brothers, Shakespeare—and reveled in the speakeasy hubbub in which my mother's bartender brother was much admired for his skill as a mixologist.

The presumption that they escaped their ancestors' world—a chronicle of unhappy endings that culminated in starvation and migration—was rocked by the Crash of '29 and the Great Depression. My mother lost her small savings as a teacher when the Edgewater Savings Bank folded. Her immigrant father lost his life savings, the accumulation of forty years working in a brewery. Pensionless, he worked until he died. My two aunts, one a teacher, the other a secretary, stayed unwed and at home to support my grandmother.

Though he had an engineering and law degree, my father struggled to find a fulltime job. He volunteered with the local Democratic Club. Edward J. Flynn, the formidable Fordham-educated leader (AKA "The Boss") of the Bronx Democratic organization and a confidante of Governor Franklin Roosevelt, took a liking to him. Flynn sent my father to the 1932 Democratic convention to Chicago as part of a contingent that worked behind the scenes to keep the New York delegation in line for FDR. He campaigned hard for FDR, speaking around the city from the back of a flatbed truck. In 1936, he was elected to the State Assembly. A week after the election, eight years after they met, my parents were married.

My father spent the rest of his life in Bronx politics, serving in the assembly until 1944, then a term in the U.S. Congress (he was one of the two congressmen from New York who rode FDR's funeral train to Hyde Park), and the rest of his career as a judge of the Municipal Court, chief judge of the City Court, and a justice of the State Supreme Court. He was at home in the Bronx, in the parish in which he grew up.

His obituary in the *New York Times* states that his "associates described him as a witty and brilliant man who loved to sing Irish songs and tell Irish stories." My father and mother were both fine singers and dancers. The songs were mainly from Broadway shows or the Great American Song Book, the dances foxtrots and waltzes, not reels and jigs. The "Irish songs" weren't folk tunes but Irish-American favorites like "Harrigan," "Galway Bay," and their all-time favorite, "How Are Things in Glocca Morra?" (lyrics by Jewish songwriter, E.Y. Harberg). The stories my father excelled at telling—stories salted with theatrical mastery of dialects—rarely involved Ireland (when they did, they were ghost stories) and rose instead from his life amid the mishegas of Bronx politics.

I took for granted that the Irish-American world my family existed in for over a century would remain as it was. The election of John F. Kennedy as president in 1960 felt like a capstone. Shortly before the election, Kennedy spoke at the Concourse Plaza. My father, running in his last election for the state Supreme Court, also spoke. Afterwards, Kennedy traveled up the Grand Course on the back of a convertible, a quaintly distant, pre-Dallas image. My friends and I stood in front of the Loew's Paradise, a movie palace since stripped and defaced, and helped swell the pan-ethnic delirium that arose when Kennedy mounted a platform in front of long-vanished Sachs Furniture and Krum's Candy stores.

Permanence of any kind is the grandest of illusions. What was different about the Bronx was the velocity with which the illusion crumbled. The origins of the Bronx as one of the city's five boroughs (the only one on the U.S. mainland) were obscure even to Bronxites. I heard passing mention among my elders of "annexation" and "consolidation," but the hardedge, unremitting brick-on-brick streetscapes disguised its overnight transformation from pastoral to metropolitan and made it seem pretty much the same since the Dutch forcibly evicted the peaceable, innocent Lenapes.

The centrifugal swirl that memory insists descended suddenly, like a fast-moving storm, had been building for some time. The pharaonic schemes of nonpareil powerbroker Robert Moses carried traffic around and across the Bronx to Long island and New Jersey. The fund-starved, once-efficient public transit system creaked and sputtered. FHA mortgages spurred the upwardly mobile, suburban aspirations of would-be homeowners and at the same time maintained and abetted the legacy of residential apartheid that condemned minorities to a decaying, substandard housing stock.

Economic change drove social change, and reinforced it. Vatican II altered our unalterable church. Priests and nuns molted back into civilians. Parishioners moved away. Once-thriving parishes became enfeebled. Rock 'n' roll and the sexual revolution made the generation gap seem more a chasm. Crime and fear of it escalated. The Concourse Plaza became a welfare hotel. The celluloid Bronx of *Marty* and *A Catered Affair*, the home of good-hearted working-class stiffs, descended into *Fort Apache, the Bronx*, a crime-ridden wasteland ruled by drug addicts and crooked cops. Formerly a synonym for low-rent blah, the borough was now "the burning Bronx," a global synecdoche for urban ruin.

The future fled the Bronx. Friends moved away or never returned from college. Soon enough I followed, serving as a VISTA volunteer in Kansas City. Beckoned by the beautiful and new—everything the Bronx wasn't—I felt the lure of California. It was then, for the first time, I thought about what I was leaving behind: the saga of the Atlantic passover from poverty and subservience to steerage and immigrant tenements; those who made it, those who didn't, those whose names I knew, those I didn't. I turned my footsteps home and returned to New York.

I attended Bronx Catholic institutions from kindergarten to the last stages of a PhD. Though they were all founded or largely staffed by Irish and Irish Americans, my first encounter with Irish history was in a college course on Victorian Britain. The past was a blur. It was as if we emerged from the shadows and fully entered history when we came to the Bronx.

My threadbare connection to Michael Manning, my great-grandfather, was my father's memory of him as an old, blind man, quiet and gentle, who never alluded to what led him to emigrate other than to say that he would never think about going back "until they hanged the last landlord." Except that he was born in pre-famine Ireland and emigrated before the Civil

War, all I knew of him was a line in the census—occupation: laborer—and the place of his death on January 10, 1910, 296 East 7th Street, a long-ago demolished tenement. I later learned the name Manning was an errant transcription of Mangan that, for whatever reason, stuck. The rest was silence.

When I returned to New York, any research I did was lackadaisical and accidental. So was my career. I worked as a Wall Street messenger, a court officer in Bronx Landlord & Tenant Court, archivist at the New York Botanical Gardens (natives always refer to it as the *Bronx* Botanical Gardens), et al., until I found my way to a graduate program at Fordham. I was a graduate assistant to the late Maurice O'Connell, a scholar of Irish history and descendant of Daniel O'Connell, the Liberator, a towering figure in that history.

I traveled to Ireland and studied there. Though I felt an intimate connection to the land and people, I confronted the fact it wasn't home and I didn't belong. On one occasion, I took my mother to her father's village. Not a trace of the family remained. The journey my ancestors made was final and irreversible. Caught on the hyphen between this small island to the east and the vast continent to the west, I recognized that my native land was the interspace on America's Atlantic ledge.

Why the past means so much to some and not much—or not at all—to others is hard to figure. At bottom, I think, it involves history as therapy, as a key to understanding self as well as society, as a restless desire to uncover what we don't know about ourselves, however partial or fractured that must be. Perhaps that hope was best captured by New York novelist and memoirist Kathleen Hill when she writes, "our journey toward understanding the selves we had considered lost forever or, worse, have never even missed, may be restored if we are patiently attentive to our inner promptings."

In the early morning hours and in the time I could game or

grift from my corporate day job, I began trying to reconstruct what I could of my ancestors' immigrant world. It gradually dawned on me that the history I sought belonged to lives too unimportant to record, people who suffered history rather than recorded it, servants, laborers, anonymous poor, ordinary moments that weren't written anywhere, the intricate tangle of existences shrunk to generalities, statistics, accidental mention, a census line.

Despairing of history, I decided to venture into the terra incognita of fiction and attempt a novel set during the Civil War Draft Riots, an epic explosion—part race riot, part insurrection—that tore New York City apart and exposed the perennial, often-feral struggle among those at the bottom of American society.

I copied paragraphs from novels I admired, scribbled the beginnings of the story I wanted to tell. I researched, wrote, despaired, rewrote, deserted, returned, persisted across an entire decade. I discovered in fiction truths I didn't in history. I grappled with the power of the past to bolt in place the unconscious exoskeleton that supported and shaped—sometimes misshaped—expectations and relationships far into the future. I came to grasp the human need to forget as well as remember. I learned that what goes unspoken, unacknowledged, has the greatest sway of all. Everything around me, parish, school, politics, religion, the Bronx I grew up in and carry with me, sprang from and contained what came before. The past never goes away, I realized, only ignored or denied.

My characters became my companions, comrades-in-arms, soulmates, a company of aspiring, compromised, lustful, decent, cowardly, ruthless, compassionate, befuddled human beings—Irish, African-Americans, old-stock New Yorkers—that I gathered under a phrase from a prayer I said since childhood: "banished children of eve." Some were imaginary, some reconstructed from random facts and fragments inherited from my family, some like Stephen Foster and John Hughes, real.

I listened as they mumbled, murmured, shouted, revealed themselves. They prompted me, guided me, led me through the vale of tears and weeping, laughter and rejoicing that each generation travels in its own way. They gave me back the past and reminded me of what I thought I didn't know. They taught me that the borders of our native land are the borders of our hearts.

# Maeve Brennan

*(January 6, 1917–November 1, 1993)*

No other female Irish writer in New York has garnered the mythical status of Dublin-born Maeve Brennan. It's no surprise that in the years since her death in 1993, Maeve's star has continued to ascend. Her life story played out like a Greek tragedy, full of artistic brilliance, unrequited love, and the insanity that destroyed her.

It has been suggested that Brennan may have been the inspiration for the character Holly Golightly in Truman Capote's "Breakfast at Tiffany's." (Brennan and Capote worked together at both *The New Yorker* and *Harper's Bazaar*.) It's doubtful Brennan would have objected to the comparison. She was a writer acutely aware of her own public persona. Maeve Brennan made a career out of creating Maeve Brennan. It was a creation so elaborate, it's possible that in the end she lost sight of what was real and what had been imagined.

Maeve was conceived out of the 1916 Easter Rising, born in Dublin on January 6, 1917. Her Nationalist Republican parents, Robert and Una Brennan, took part in the Rising in March 1916. Robert was sentenced to death, but the sentence was commuted to penal servitude. Maeve was born while he was in prison. In 1934, her father founded *The Irish Press,* and later that same year he moved the family to Washington when he was appointed the Irish Free State's first minister to the United States.

After her parents returned to Ireland in 1947, twenty-year-old Maeve stayed on in New York, finding work as a fashion copywriter at *Harper's Bazaar.* Then, in 1949, William Shawn noticed a short piece she wrote for *The New Yorker* and offered her a staff writing position with the magazine.

It was at *The New Yorker* that Brennan found her voice, writing sketches under the pseudonym "The Long-Winded Lady." The following year, *The New Yorker* began to publish her short stories also. Friends and work associates at *The New Yorker* described Brennan as petite, intelligent, and stylish; she wore a freshly cut flower, usually a rose, on the lapel of her perfectly tailored work jacket each day. She was also undeniably eccentric and moved from room to rented room like a woman hell bent on trying to outrun herself.

Maeve Brennan was writing at a time when few Irish women were brave enough to do so. The very act of writing was an affront to the conservative secular society she had left behind in Ireland. She never felt comfortable returning home again. Her work was widely read in the United States during the fifties and sixties, but even though most of her stories were set in her hometown of Dublin, she remained practically unheard of in her own country.

In those early years at *The New Yorker*, she fell madly in love with theater critic Walter Kerr, who broke her heart when he ended their engagement to marry someone else. It was a heartbreak she never seemed to recover from. She married fellow *New Yorker* writer St. Clair McKelway. McKelway was an erratic drunk, and it was becoming obvious that Brennan's own mental state was beginning to fray at the seams. The marriage fell apart after two tumultuous years.

After the marriage, there were fits and starts, but it was becoming apparent to those around her that Brennan was troubled. Her mysterious, brittle glamour began to fray at the seams. By the early 1970s, she had become a paranoid alcoholic. She was hospitalized numerous times during this period. It became impossible for her to maintain any sort of stability in her life, though she continued to write short fictional pieces for the magazine and to bounce from rented to room to room. She finally wound up sleeping in an unused cubical next to the women's bathroom at *The New Yorker*. When she got paid, she could be seen standing in Times Square handing out dollar bills to passing strangers. On arriving at the office one morning during this time, workers were alarmed to find that Brennan had trashed the place during the night, smashing glass-paneled doors and picture frames. William Maxwell and a few others combined efforts to have her hospitalized.

After receiving treatment and medication at University Hospital, she stabilized again for a spell and even returned to Ireland in 1973 for the first time in thirty-nine years, where she stayed in a small cottage behind the family house of a fifteen-year-old Roddy Doyle. Doyle's mother, Ita, was Brennan's cousin. The reports of Brennan's erratic behavior during this trip suggest that she gave up her medication once she began to feel her health return. By 1974 she was back in New York.

Brennan's decline was a slow and painful ordeal. Her fellow work staff were at a loss for what to do with her. She had become enmeshed in the life of the magazine through a series of ill-fated romantic entanglements, and now they felt a need to shelter her from the inevitable fall for as long as they could. But Maeve's mental illness had taken hold, and there was nothing anyone could do to stop the decline.

In 1976, a new Plexiglas front was erected at the receptionist's desk, and the staff was given strict instructions not to grant Brennan entry for fear of violence. In her biography of Brennan, *Homesick at The New Yorker,* Angela Bourke writes that in 1981 an editor arrived to work one morning at the magazine "to find a very small woman, in a long untidy black skirt, with grey, unwashed hair, sitting in silence outside the Plexiglas partition staring at the floor. She sat there until evening and returned the next day." It was the last noted sighting of Brennan at the *New Yorker* office.

After that, there were ghostly sightings of Brennan here and there around Manhattan, but she was drifting into the unknown. The writer Edith Konecky, who was a close friend of Brennan's during this time, tried desperately to help her find stability in a residence, but it was too late. Maeve would disappear overnight, leaving no indication of which seedy Times Square hotel she had fled to. At some time during this period, she was admitted to Lawrence Nursing Home in Far Rockaway, Queens. She died of a heart attack there on November 1, 1993, at the age of seventy-six. Not a single Irish newspaper printed an obituary. Maeve had yet to be discovered.

Colin Broderick

# Luanne Rice

Luanne Rice is the *New York Times* best-selling author of thirty-four novels, translated into twenty-four languages. Several of her novels have been adapted for television, and her work has been featured at Hartford Stage, the Geffen Playhouse, and off-Broadway. Many of her novels deal with the mysteries of an Irish-American upbringing, with characters returning to Dublin, Cork, Wicklow, and Dungannon to track down the family ghosts. She moved to Chelsea after dropping out of college to write, and although she's lived other places through the years, she's never really left.

# Wine Comes in at the Mouth

Starting when I was ten, my father would take me to New York late at night. He'd park our Ford station wagon in a narrow lane under the hulking West Side Highway at the tip of Manhattan. He said we were sweethearts and partners. The streets were dark, full of shadows from skyscrapers and the elevated roadway, and he locked me into the car while he went into 90 West Street.

I sat low in the seat to stay invisible. Across West Street were wharves, and the oily black Hudson River flowing into the Atlantic, and my father said a lot of the dockworkers were Irish from Ireland, and to tell them I was Irish Catholic if anyone bothered me. He said even Catholics could be rape artists, but usually not.

He was in there so long my heart wanted to explode. Was he ever coming back? Was he having affairs with the secretaries? But secretaries wouldn't be working at night, would they? I was a tiny, jealous ten-year-old wife. At home in Connecticut, he took me on lots of service calls, but this was a pickup. We were at the United States home office for Olympia typewriters.

He sold and repaired them. They were German, and he always apologized for that, having been a decorated navigator-bombardier in World War II, shot down after bombing Dresden, but he said Germans made the best machinery, you couldn't argue with fact. Many nights he stayed out drinking, he didn't come home. He was angular and handsome, with a tortured, war-torn soul, irresistible to ladies who liked unavailable husbands and fathers, so on the way down to New York I would tell him reasons he should be with our family at night, and not run around, and he would seem to agree. But he always stayed out again. I pictured him with the answering-service lady. He couldn't afford a secretary, but he had an answering service, and her voice sounded tempting and sexy. Even as a child I had an ear for seduction.

Alone in the car, I worried more about what my father was doing up in the skyscraper than what might happen to me. The alley was mostly deserted, but people walked behind the car on West Street, shadows slashing between streetlamps. I'd watch till they passed out of sight, and wonder where they were going.

I had a notebook with me at all times, and I would find the place in the car where a tiny sliver of light slanted in from one of the building windows. I would contort to keep myself hidden in the dark but my pad in the light and write stories and poems about happy families whose parents never fought.

Vigilant for my father, I would jump when he returned. I'd unlock the car door, and he'd lower the tailgate and fill the station wagon with crated Olympia typewriters, manual and electric. Then we'd drive back to New Britain. I would pretend to have a sore throat and stay home from school the next day, and I'd finish the stories started under the West Side Highway.

I generally missed about half of every school year, due to various made-up maladies and late nights either waiting up for my father or accompanying him on typewriter runs. Our family always seemed ready to break. Shy at school, I felt I didn't fit in with normal kids. I'd rather stay home and live in my imagination. The trips to New York haunted my dreams, the dark streets exerted a pull on me.

*The New Yorker* was our family bible. My mother read to us from the magazine at bedtime, and I dreamed of having a story in it when I got older. After I dropped out of college for my first bad depression, I began to submit my work. Mostly I got rejection slips on heavy bond cream-colored paper with a small black Eustace Tilley imprinted at the top, but when I was nineteen, I got a personal letter from Brendan Gill. He had taken note of the fact my short stories about an Irish-American family were set in Connecticut, where he was from, and he invited me to New York for lunch.

Brendan, the drama critic at *The New Yorker,* was also of Irish descent. What to wear filled me with angst. I didn't have anything sophisticated enough. I borrowed a dress from the mother of the kids I babysat for and I cut the brass buttons off my grandfather's Hartford Police Department jacket—they bore the seal of the City of Hartford, where Brendan had grown up, I thought he might like that—and sewed them onto my high school uniform blazer.

I took the train down. Brendan didn't notice the buttons. He poured me a glass of Pouilly-Fuissé at the Hideaway—a small space he rented at 25 West Forty-third Street, a few floors up from the magazine offices. There he told me, sitting on a black leather couch, that as a young writer I needed to know three things: Read Yeats and commit his poems to memory; have a happy life and don't become depressed and alcoholic like Maeve Brennan; get and stay married; and move to New York to live a literary life.

That day he taught me *A Drinking Song,* by William Butler Yeats:

> Wine comes in at the mouth
> And love comes in at the eye;
> That's all we shall know for truth
> Before we grow old and die.
> I lift the glass to my mouth,
> I look at you, and I sigh.

Then we went to the Algonquin and sat in the booth next to William Shawn in the Rose Room. Brendan ordered us Lillets, then more wine with our chef's salads, and as I tried to remember the poem, my head spun and I wondered who was Maeve Brennan.

Did a literary life mean lunch at the Algonquin? For a while I just took the train in from Connecticut, meeting Brendan at the magazine and hand-delivering stories, none of which was accepted, to the fiction department. But the headiness of being there, being introduced to literary luminaries like William Maxwell and Penelope Gilliatt, seeing sketches by James Thurber, made me feel this was the life I wanted to live, that if I stayed close enough, maybe my work would make it into the pages.

I moved to New York, a room in a boardinghouse on Tenth Avenue in Chelsea. The owner was Irish and looked friendly and somewhat jolly like my uncle Bill, but he used his wife's surname instead of his own, and that seemed mysterious. There was a bar on the first floor where workmen in plaid shirts and construction boots drank at one end and guys who wore leather jackets and spoke in brogues drank at the other.

The neighborhood, not yet gentrified, was full of warehouses and parking lots. I wanted to drink like a writer. Since alcoholics were old and wore filthy raincoats and drank all day, I didn't have to worry as long as I didn't start before six. The Irish guys at the far end of the bar would stand me a drink and flirt. I'd ask what brought them to New York, but they didn't like to answer questions. They'd ask me where my people were from, back in Ireland. I said Dublin and Wicklow, and Timoleague, in Cork.

Eileen, a waitress, told me the Irish guys were in a gang. They were tougher than the Mafia, and they'd cut off your head if you crossed them, but we didn't have to worry because since she worked here and I lived here we were family. When not trying to fuck us, they'd protect us. And she told me the reason my landlord used his wife's name was that he had been involved in shady dealings back in Ireland and had to keep a low profile.

The streets in West Chelsea were full of S&M bars, and just past dawn each morning I'd sit at my desk facing Tenth Avenue and see men walking home in black leather and spiked collars, sometimes leading each other on chains. Prostitutes headed north from Fourteenth Street, chatting away.

I felt I had found my place and my people in this far west corner of New York City. Yet my writing continued to be set on the Connecticut shoreline, populated by WASPs who went to yacht clubs and drank gin and tonics in dew-beaded Orrefors crystal—not Waterford, that was too Irish for these characters—served on silver trays, and who led the lives I thought I should wish I did.

One rainy day, Brendan and I were walking from the Hideaway to the Algonquin, and we met a woman on West Forty-fourth Street. I sensed Brendan wanting to avoid her, but we came face-to-face. She was a ravaged beauty, with high cheekbones and bloodshot, sorrowful eyes. He introduced her as Maeve Brennan.

When we walked away, he looked at me sharply and repeated what he'd said once before: "Don't turn out like her." He told me she had come from Dublin to New York with hopes, dreams, and wild talent, that she had written short stories and appeared in the magazine as "the Long-Winded Lady," and had fallen into the bottle. Then we went in to lunch and drank Lillet.

I went to the library looking for Maeve's work. My branch didn't have any, so I went to the Jefferson Market Branch in the Village, searched back issues of *The New Yorker*. Her stories were so beautiful and bereft, they gave me goose bumps and made me cry.

I thought of Brendan's warning and knew, in some deep and secret part of myself, that I was just like Maeve: not in talent, but in heart and sadness. I told myself that being Irish was a big part of the problem. It was mixed up in my mind with my father's drinking, secrets, family anguish, and the Catholicism I had always treated, to zero effect, as a Ouija board and a wishing well.

I told myself I wasn't an alcoholic, that the drinking I did—Jamesons with the guys on Tenth Avenue, Pouilly-Fuissé and Lillet with Brendan at the Hideaway and the Algonquin and the Century—was because I was a writer. But maybe Maeve had once thought that, too, and inside I knew: I was like her.

My father died of cancer. I was drinking alone, too depressed to get up in the morning. One summer weekend, I returned to Connecticut, wanting to crawl home to some kind of comfort and a return to innocence. There I met the man who would be my first husband. He was kind, studious, nothing like the Irish gang guys, and nothing like my father. Life with him took me away from New York for a while—to Washington, D.C., where he attended law school; Providence, Rhode Island; Paris; then back to New York.

I wrote my first novel while married to him. I wrote it in longhand, on yellow legal pads. When my husband took the New York bar-review course at Town Hall, around the corner from the Algonquin on West Forty-third Street, I'd accompany him to each lecture and sit in the theater balcony and write while the professors spoke about torts and contracts. I'd tune out the law and live in the world of my fiction.

Staying close to my husband was key. He wasn't like my father, but I didn't know how he might change, start running around, drinking and cheating. If I dropped my guard, anything might happen. I cooked him fancy meals every night, even when he had to work late, like all Wall Street law firm associates. Sometimes we had dinner at one in the morning, sometimes at three.

I got up early and wrote straight through the day, but the closer I got to six o'clock, the worse I felt. That was the witching hour. As a kid, I knew my father would be home by six or not at all. I would go into the bedroom I shared with my two younger sisters and kneel by the window, my knees bare on the hard oak floor, aching in a sort of suburban hair-shirt martyrdom, giving up my sore knees to Mary, to whom I prayed that my father would come home, that he wouldn't die or kill someone in a drunken crash, that he wouldn't fall in love with whatever woman he was with, that my parents wouldn't get divorced. Even in New York, with a husband who loved me and was nothing like my father, six o'clock had a dark, sick power over me.

We lived at One Gramercy Park, on the fourth floor of a townhouse with a fireplace and a key to the park. It was romantic and idyllic, at tree level, and had no air-conditioning. On summer nights, we would open the windows and Lexington Avenue nightclub traffic would dead-end at the park, and we'd lie awake to the blare of horns. I got used to drinking myself to sleep and to blocking out feelings that were starting to surface, that troubled me: He was the right guy, but I was the wrong girl.

My first novel was *Angels All Over Town*. Massively hungover, I typed one draft on my old Olympia, but when it came time for my agent to submit, I went down to a typing studio in the shadow of the World Trade Center, where IBM Selectrics were available for ten dollars a day. I'd sit in the studio, school-type desks filled with people typing term papers, trying to increase their typing speed, and one man who looked like the cliché of a tortured writer, with a black turtleneck, raking his beard with one hand while talking about his novel to anyone who sat near him. I sat far away and finished retyping the four-hundred-page draft in five days.

My agent submitted it to publishers. I met her the same year I got married, and she has been the love of my life. Our relationship has lasted longer than any of my three marriages. I feel closer to her than to almost anyone in the world, including the sister who has estranged herself from me. But back then we were relatively new, and we weren't to know that we would make magic together—thirty-two books, twenty-four translations, five movies and counting as I write this.

*Angels* was accepted by Atheneum. It was about a young Irish-American woman whose alcoholic father appears to her as a ghost. Their surname is Cavan, after the county in Ireland, and one of her ancestors was a stonemason who worked on Saint Patrick's in Dungannon, just as one of mine did. My aunts hated the portrayal of the father, who they took to be modeled after mine.

He was, in a way. And my father's ghost haunted me. On weekends while my husband spent inevitable hours slogging through public offerings at 53 Wall Street, I'd walk over to West Street. I'd try to remember being ten, waiting for my father. The elevated highway had been torn down, the wharves demolished to create Battery Park City, and the Twin Towers built. It was so changed, hard to find a memory of those midnights by the docks.

But they would come to me at night, in our perfect Gramercy Park apartment. I started drinking before six. And I'd keep it up all night. One time my husband came home at one, and I didn't have dinner ready. He was surprised, but I think he was glad.

He went to sleep. I took a bottle of Scotch and climbed halfway out the window. I sat there looking out at Gramercy Park, still and quiet in the middle of the night. I thought about jumping, but figured four stories wasn't enough to kill me. My husband was too nice. It wasn't going to work. I took a slug from the bottle and knew I was going to leave.

Frank McCourt (right) with his brother Malachy.

# Frank McCourt

*(August 19, 1930–July 19, 2009)*

Once in a blue moon, a book comes along that rocks the publishing world to its core, a book that redefines a generation or a genre. In 1996, that book was *Angela's Ashes*. *Angela's Ashes* was different from any autobiography that had come before it. It didn't read like a book—it read like a yarn being spun, over a hot cup of tea, in front of a turf fire. The voice was at once playful, reflective, and 100 percent accessible. Its complete lack of literary pretension was practically a mortal sin in Irish letters. How did this commoner find his way to the table? Who was this young ruffian who'd so startled half-sleeping editors all over town?

For a start, he was no youngster, except of course in spirit.

Frank McCourt was sixty-six when he blasted onto the scene. It turns out he'd already been busy changing lives for decades, as a high school teacher in New York City.

He was born into the Great Depression, in Brooklyn, on 19 August 1930, the oldest son of Angela and Malachy McCourt. McCourt's account of childhood misery would become legendary. With one infamous line, he practically cornered the market in hardship:

"Worse than the ordinary miserable childhood is the miserable Irish childhood, and worse yet is the miserable Irish Catholic childhood."

The details of his early life are stark and painful to consider. Frank was one of six siblings, three of whom would die in early childhood from the squalor of their living conditions. Margaret, the youngest, died just weeks after childbirth in Brooklyn. Twin boys Oliver and Eugene died soon after the family moved back to a cold, damp slum in Limerick. Frank was just eleven when his alcoholic father abandoned the family, leaving Angela to fend for herself.

No one ever becomes accustomed to poverty, to flea-ridden mattresses, to hunger, to cold and damp living conditions. For the young Frank, it was a childhood endured.

By the age of nineteen, McCourt was back living in New York. He was a boy determined never to return to that squalor again. Once back on American soil, he worked a series of menial jobs, cleaning lavatories at the Biltmore Hotel, stacking boxes in a warehouse. Before long he was drafted into the U.S. Army during the Korean War, where he proved himself a reliable soldier, rising up through the ranks to become colonel. Afterwards, McCourt used the GI bill to put himself through college, emerging from NYU with a bachelor's degree in 1957 and a master's degree from Brooklyn College in 1967.

For the next thirty years, Frank McCourt taught in one New

York high school after another.

In his mid-fifties, he began to dabble in writing. In 1985 he premiered a two-man show, *A Couple of Blaguards,* which he co-wrote with his brother Malachy. The pair performed the show around the U.S. for years and even traveled back to perform in their hometown of Limerick. But it wasn't until he retired from teaching in 1987 that McCourt began to write about his life in earnest. He wrote *Angela's Ashes, 'Tis,* and *Teacher Man* in quick succession, and over the course of just a few years won a Pulitzer Prize, a National Book Critics Circle Award, and the *Los Angeles Times* Book Award.

*Newsweek* described *Angela's Ashes* as "the publishing industry's Cinderella story of the decade." The book shot to number one on the *New York Times* best-seller list. It was translated into more than twenty languages. In 1998 Frank McCourt was elected Irish-American of the Year by *Irish America* magazine.

When asked about the development of his writing style in a *Toronto Sun* interview in 2000, McCourt replied, "When you stand before 170 teenagers each day, you have to get and keep their attention. Their attention span is about seven minutes, which is the time between commercials. So you have to stay on your toes."

In early 2009, McCourt was being treated for melanoma. By July 19, he was gone.

Colin Broderick

# Larry Kirwan

Larry Kirwan was leader of Black 47 for 25 years. He has written 15 plays and musicals, three novels, a memoir and A History of Irish Music. He writes a bi-weekly column for *The Irish Echo* and hosts *Celtic Crush* on SiriusXM. He is president of Irish American Writers & Artists.

# Alphabet City

She was the most beautiful woman I had ever seen. Long brown hair with a trace of chestnut, black eyes flashing, usually with disdain; she moved like a dancer, the space shifting before and after her. She was Puerto Rican and I never spoke to her—you didn't unless you were introduced. That was the scene at the Kiwi, an after-hours club on East Ninth between First and Avenue A. It had its own set of rules and etiquette, and you followed them precisely if you knew what was good for you.

Her name was Carlita—Jimmy Reece told me that. He said she was bad news, keep away from her, and I did, because Jimmy Reece knew the score on everyone in the Kiwi. He was a cool black dude who watched everything and was accepted by everyone. I envied the casual way he spoke to Carlita, but he didn't seem much interested in women, although he couldn't have been a whole lot more than fifty at the time. Reece had taken me under his wing. Every now and again he'd order me to "go home, get some sleep, tomorrow is another day," and all the other clichés that no one else would tell you in a grungy after-hours.

The Kiwi floated in a separate universe: It stayed open twenty-four hours and was windowless, so time did its own thing within those sweat-stained, Sheetrock walls. Carlita was a law unto her own, too, she just seemed to materialize from out of the blue, but I swear the minute she opened the door, the smoky air changed. Everyone knew she'd entered. You could feel the pressure drop, but most everyone was too cool to acknowledge her, except for Reece, and Maria, the tall, trashy, platinum-blond transvestite who tended bar.

Carlita only showed when Roman was there. He was her boyfriend, a burly, arrogant Ukrainian who occupied the far corner of the bar where the light was dimmest. Roman was married. I used to see him stroll around Tomkins Square Park with his wife and two children on Sunday afternoons. He never acknowledged me on those outings. But I had other reasons not to like Roman.

I didn't know it then, but Jesus didn't care much for him, either. I was afraid of Jesus, a midlevel smack dealer from the projects on Avenue D. He never smiled, and why should he? With a gig like his, you had to have icicles coursing through your veins. He was impossibly handsome in that Latino way—olive skin, perfect features, pitch-black oily hair combed back. He always wore a suit, a pressed white shirt, and a razor-thin tie. I had no idea that he too was sleeping with Carlita—until the Sunday morning that changed everything.

That's when the Kiwi door came flying in, almost off its hinges, and the big redheaded cop from the Ninth Precinct slammed his nightstick down on the bar, yelling, "You fucking scum!"

The music blared on, the stale smoke hung in blue ridges, but we were struck with silence—trying to put two and two together while the hostile daylight streamed in the open doorway.

He slammed the nightstick down one more time for emphasis. "Get out on that fucking street!"

Jimmy Reece was the first on his feet and I was barely a beat behind him. A couple of Ricans visiting from Bayamón beat us into the street and blocked our way. We sidled around them and my stomach lurched at the sight of Roman lying there near the gutter, a neat surgical rip in his blood-covered shirt, eyes closed forever, three old Ukrainian ladies lighting candles around him, chanting some guttural prayers, but no tears limning their overwhelming sadness.

The crowd of drinkers pushed past us, squinting into the sun-bleached morning—not a syllable out of the rowdiest of them.

Not even a murmur; it was like we were all trapped in a silent movie until the redheaded cop spoke, quietly, resignedly, "You couldn't leave well enough the fuck alone, could you?"

It was then Jimmy Reece elbowed me gently and nodded across the street. Carlita had emerged from the shadow of an awning. She paused for one last look, then, dry-eyed but determined, turned east for the projects on Avenue D.

How much of the above is true? Remarkably, much of it. Some of the names have been changed, some of the events rearranged, but it's a heightened slice of life from New York City in the wild and woolly 1970s. There was a Carlita, and I still think of her raw beauty and bearing, though I daresay she's a grandmother now—if she's alive. Jimmy Reece was a lovely man who arrived in the Kiwi straight after work every Friday night, carrying a suitcase that contained his toiletries and multiple changes of clothing. Apart from some visits to a friend's apartment for showers or a turn around Tomkins Square for his daily constitutional, he sat on the same stool all weekend—occasionally resting his head on the counter while grabbing a nap—until heading home to Harlem Sunday night to rest up for the workweek.

He hated dealers and junkies with a passion, for "the horse killed the Bird," that's how he spoke, with no concession to the unhip—"the horse" was heroin, "the Bird," Charlie Parker. He also opened up my early-twenties, constipated, know-it-all Irish brain to the magic of John Coltrane, a gift I'll always treasure. Then again, he had a little help in that department, for when you entered the Kiwi, you were handed a bottle of cold Heineken and two joints for a five-dollar bill; the price was actually four dollars, but a tip of a buck for Maria was deemed de rigeur.

I was the only Paddy who frequented the place, one of the few gringos, for that matter. I had gained membership because I lived in a dump across the street where the boiler broke down frequently. When you complained, the owner encouraged you to spend the frigid hours at the Kiwi. It was the perfect place to learn about writing, for one was a guest in a house of many cultures, and there was a sore need for silence, cunning, and active awareness. The latter aptitude, or developed skill, is essential for any writer. When you listen, you become aware; not only do you decipher speech patterns and the gist of stories, you also learn to delineate and appreciate character. The actual interactions between characters are rarely as important as the characters themselves.

Although I've used the above story about Carlita in the Black 47 song *Blood Wedding,* should I ever choose to turn the raw data into a novel or play, I would already be well ahead of the game because I can see and hear the characters. I acquired that skill by observing the denizens of the Kiwi on countless after-hours nights.

I spent just as many evenings in Malachy McCourt's Bells of Hell saloon, but I picked up fewer skills there. I was more of a player, talking and laughing aimlessly among such eloquent characters as my host, his brother Frank and mother Angela, and friends and acquaintances the like of Lester Bangs, David Amram, and, on occasion, Joe Strummer and Joey Ramone. But there's nothing like solitary listening to catch the particular tone and character of a person.

New York in the 1970s was a playground, albeit a violent one. As long as you kept your nose reasonably clean, the cops let you be what you were, or, even more important, what you had designs on becoming. You could reinvent yourself overnight and no one gave a goddamn. I had sore need of such a makeover after having grown up in the womblike town of Wexford, where everyone knew your business and had a fixed idea of who and what you were. My friend, the playwright Billy Roche, was able to transcend Wexford's amniotic claustrophobia by illuminating it—much as Blake could pinpoint the universe in a grain of sand. I couldn't, and so I had to get out.

I left to find my voice. Ah, the voice! Until you find it, you're basically treading water as a writer, picking up some necessary skills, of course—and you'll need those—but it's the voice that counts. Miles Davis put it best: "I could stare at a picture and come up with a thousand notes that would replicate it, but it wasn't until I found my voice that I could go beyond it."

I didn't find mine until we formed Black 47. Perhaps it was because I'd apprenticed in three different disciplines—songwriter, playwright, and novelist—or maybe I'm just a painfully slow learner. I had found aspects of my voice early on and had some success as a musician and playwright, but something was missing, and I felt it keenly. I even walked away from music for years, appalled by my lack of originality. I didn't think I'd ever return. In retrospect, though, I was "going to the mountain." That's a necessary part of the creative process. Just walking away from it all, giving your mind and soul time to catch up and adjust.

And in that time, I became a playwright. I lived and breathed the craft—and it is a craft, notice how the last six letters spell *wright*. Just before I made the break, I stumbled upon a good idea—what would have happened to the Beatles if they hadn't made it? I joined a group called Script Development Workshop, where you could bring in a play, work on it with a director and a group of actors, then put it on stage for an evening and have your fellow participants critique it.

At the time, my band, Major Thinkers, had a deal with Epic Records and our career was booming. I was close to Cyndi Lauper, who was signed to the same label. I had agreed to be in a video for a catchy song of hers, "Girls Just Want to Have Fun." It was to be shot all day one Sunday, but my play was being mounted that Monday night, and it needed a serious overhaul.

I decided to cancel my video appearance and concentrate on the play. Of course I had no idea that "Girls" would become one of the most popular MTV videos ever. Another great Kirwan career decision! I never regretted my choice, though, for I knew I was onto something with *Liverpool Fantasy*. It caused an uproar that Monday night at Script Development Workshop, with many loathing the play while others championed a "new voice." It's had many productions since then and is perennially talked of as a potential movie; besides, I eventually made my own MTV videos, so I suppose it all worked out for the best.

Within a year, Major Thinkers was dropped by Epic! I walked away from the music business and became a full-time playwright. Though penniless, I was a happy man, for I was on my way to finding my voice.

My friends looked at me askance. I was giving up something I'd devoted so many years to. I survived a number of interventions and soulful 4:00 a.m. heart-to-heart talks, but they made no difference. For I had learned something invaluable down all the years of hustling—take no advice. That might seem bullheaded and counterintuitive, but in reality it's just common sense. Instincts are the compass that will guide you, and they must be developed—often at a price. You'll make huge mistakes striking off on your own, but there's no other way to develop your intuition and, dare I say it, your voice and character.

Nor can fear of failure be entertained. A critical disaster may be debilitating in a town the size of Wexford; but one can take a drubbing from *The New York Times*, retire to one's apartment with a bottle of Jameson's, and by the time you emerge, pale-faced and bleary-eyed, the brouhaha will have, for the most part, been forgotten. Yesterday's news tends to be of little importance in a buzzing metropolis.

As a self-employed artist—no matter what the field—you will be called upon to make decisions, artistic and otherwise,

53

on a daily basis. You have to be able to make these—often in a split second—and live with the consequences. You usually can't take the time to call someone, and besides, anyone with enough experience to help you will be in the midst of making their own decisions on difficult matters. One thing you will develop is a heightened sense of awareness—I can feel a dozen problems even now barreling down the pike towards me; hopefully some will get diverted and I'll never have to deal with them. But that's an artist's life, and unless you can make quick judgments, you're likely to get bowled over any minute of the day.

John Kuhlman was one of the finest composers I ever worked with, but though I loved him dearly, he drove me around the goddamned bend. After playing a beautiful piece, he would immediately try and better it; after three or four such attempts, he would gaze off into the near distance and murmur, "This could go a lot of different ways." At first I would stare off in tandem with him, wishing that I could come up with just one of his wonderful choices. After some days of this meandering, however, I was forced to retort in typical Paddy philistine manner, "Yeah right, John, but just pick one of the fucking things. Otherwise we could be sitting here until the balls fall off the Christmas tree!"

Make your decisions and swing for the fences. You can always discard them and start from scratch. Successful art is all about being brave and making choices. It's also about being able to take a shot straight on the chin, picking yourself up from the floor, and jumping right back into the fray. Don't be precious. Don't get stuck in a rut. Work on two or three things at the same time. The strongest will rule, but the more sublime will often benefit from the general energy created.

I wear three caps—songwriter, playwright, and novelist. You could even divide those further, for I also perform, write musicals, turn out a column for *The Irish Echo,* and host and produce Celtic Crush for SiriusXM Radio. With each, I've served long and often painful apprenticeships. I never went to school for any of them but was forced to learn the hard way—by making choices, along with copious mistakes.

You might wonder where I get the time. Well, to be honest, I live in fear of being a day late and a dollar short. New York City is an unforgiving place. It weeds out those who are unable to fend for themselves. Many of my peers have been broken by the city and its demands. Then again, artistic life reeks of disenchantment and blighted dreams. When I arrived in the city with a hundred or so dollars in my pocket, I didn't feel I could turn to my parents for money—for one thing, it was the 1970s; making a phone call to Ireland was expensive, and by the time they'd sent you the few shillings they could afford, you'd already be in the depths of some new crisis. Anyway, I was too proud and couldn't admit defeat.

Can you look poverty and rejection in the eye and still go to the pub, get hammered, and ask the best-looking girl in the house to take you home? You need a certain amount of that attitude to survive as an artist. And you better live in a place where chance can provide a break, at least one morning a week. That was New York in the seventies; that's where I learned that illogical optimism and a certain live-for-tomorrow approach is an essential part of being an artist.

You won't come to grips with that by watching television or eternally trawling the Internet. Was there ever a worse medium than television? Not only does it take up acres of your time, it coarsens your artistic nature and blunts the intellect. Turn it to the wall, only to be looked at when you need a first-class blast of masochism—then you can indulge in an inning or two of the Mets.

If you're a playwright, run a mile from the idiot box, otherwise your plays will parody sit-coms, soap operas, and all lesser dreck and dregs. If you're a novelist, you'll end up being totally obvious—the worst of fates. If you're a musician, run howling from MTV, VH1, and the late-night shows. I've been on all of them—they have nothing to do with music but offer only half-baked celebrity, another death in waiting for the serious artist, no matter how much you may long for it at times.

As for Facebook, Twitter, and all the other outlets of digitalia, use them by all means for promotion, but don't for an instant believe them. Who cares how many likes, friends, or followers you attract? They mean nothing when the chips are down and you're facing that empty sheet of paper or the guitar that's screaming to you from its dusty exile in a corner. All that matters in the long run is the creativity you can summon up. That's what makes you a writer—it's a rough furrow to plow, but if it were easy, everyone would be doing it.

The most effective of all promotional avenues is your email newsletter to those who really care about you and your career. But don't use that more than once a month—familiarity breeds contempt. There's a reason Bob Dylan, Neil Young, Thomas Keneally, and Edna O'Brien have had fifty-year careers— they've kept their mystique. Make sure you don't pawn or pimp yours away.

The artist's job is to explore the human condition, and there's one very pleasurable and easy way to do that—fall in love early and often. Here the bisexual has a tremendous advantage, for he or she can stare into the soul of both men and women; but if you're straight or unadventurous, then you'll be forced to deal in a deep way with the opposite sex, and that's important because, unless you're writing about your adventures on a desert island, you're going to have to include the other gender in your stories or songs. Of course, you're going to get burned, and often badly, but there's nothing like a good old dollop of bitterness, spiced with seasonings of regret, to nail a character or fashion a story.

Think of your favorite literary characters of the opposite sex. On this freezing afternoon, the first three that pop into my mind are Lady Brett Ashley from *The Sun Also Rises;* Justine from *The Alexandria Quartet;* and June from *Tropic of Cancer* and many of Henry Miller's other books—three very different babes, to put it mildly, and yet each had a particular effect on me at the time of reading. That's why I remember them so vividly.

Hemingway is not known for his characterization of women, and yet Lady Brett leaped out at me from *The Sun Also Rises* when I first read it in my teens. What did he capture in her character? Well, for me, it was vivacity, adventure, and a tragedy in the making. Oddly enough, when I saw the movie years later, my image of her was not unlike Ava Gardner. I would venture to suggest that whatever Hem invested in her character sparked the need I had to get out of Wexford and live a more adventurous life; but at the same time, I also recognized that once gone, I'd never fit back in again—hence the tragedy.

You are what you read, and I've read Lawrence Durrell's *Alexandria Quartet* a number of times and at different points of my life. His sentences are long, dense, and brimming with luxurious words. Durrell's loquacious Irishman, born in the Colonial Raj, poor but reeking of privilege, is the polar opposite of stark, pilgrimlike Hemingway, but what matter—a writer's taste in reading should be broad, for as Richard Thompson once said to me about guitar playing, "One should have many arrows in one's quiver, what works today may not work so well tomorrow."

Durrell spends many pages describing Justine, and yet once I put down the book, I can rarely capture an image of her. Still, I can touch, feel, smell, breathe, and inhabit her, while every time I revisit her story I learn new things about this mysterious woman. How did Durrell accomplish that? Well, he studied the woman on whom she was based for some years on a lonely

Greek island. That's what being in love does; it mists over and makes the past more than it was, and that's what writing is essentially about.

There are those who dislike Henry Miller's sex scenes. They can, I suppose, be a bit over-the-top on a hungover wet Monday morning, but there's a feral reality to them that's always gripping. And anyway, Hank eventually married his June, so you don't have to get too deep into Catholic guilt, if such be your thing. Why deal with sex, anyway, you might ask—surely it's better to allude to it rather than nail it for what it is? Well, for one thing, it's rather important to many people, and it sells. Still, as the Kerry woman was heard to say, "a little goes a long way."

Again, like Durrell, Miller spent a long time studying the love of his life, and it shows, for his June is so real, urgent, and needy, you fancy you might be in with a shot yourself if you happened to run into her on her wild nocturnal escapades around New York City. Even her skittishness and lack of dependability can be endearing, for you feel you're dealing with a flesh-and-blood woman rather than some trumped-up literary heroine.

I wonder why Molly Bloom didn't jump to my mind? Joyce studied his wife, Nora obsessively, so much so it's often hard to differentiate her reality from Molly's fiction. I daresay Molly is too demanding for me, too obsessive, too much flesh, blood, and thunder, and in the end too real, too much woman. Still, I managed to create a song to my liking from the Molly/Joyce/Nora ménage a trois. Fittingly, it's called "Molly."

You'll never be lonely as a writer, for the characters you create will perennially be knocking around in the cheap motels of your brain. Lately, for me, it's been the characters peopling *Days of Rage,* a musical I wrote more than twenty-five years ago. Perhaps that's because Stevie Hero, the protagonist, has a decision to make in the world of rock 'n'roll that somewhat mirrored my own during the disbanding of Black 47.

But if you're never lonely, you're usually quite alone. For unless you're very lucky, you'll have to inure yourself from the slings and arrows of your family, friends, and critics. In order to create, you have to change both yourself and the world around you—and that rarely sits easy with those you love and who love you. The problem with change is you're not really at your best as you're going through it.

About a year after forming, Black 47 went to London to do some dates and open for the Pogues. My mother and father came over from Wexford to see us and showed up one snowy, freezing night to some godforsaken, empty pub in North London. After an ebullient but somewhat awkward set, I joined them at their table—they never even acknowledged that I'd been onstage. It was hurtful but not meant to be that way—they "just didn't get it," and decided it was best to say nothing.

I realized then and there I'd have to cut them out of that part of my life—surely a shame, but I did it for artistic survival. In a certain way, I never went home after that. Though I loved my parents dearly and could talk to them about practically anything else, I had to erect walls around myself to safeguard my then-brittle artistic life. You'll probably have to do something of the same nature—if you haven't done so already.

And that brings us to critics. "They've spoiled many a breakfast, but never a lunch," as Noel Coward used to say. You'll need to follow that maxim. You have to develop your instincts so that you know when something is good, great, or god-awful. Because you can't rely on a critic to tell you! This can be a bit of a drag, for you're likely to get some good notices, but you can't believe them—otherwise you have to believe the bad ones, too. I rarely even read reviews anymore except to salvage a decent quote. It's essential not to put any store in them—good or bad.

One antidote is to read the theatrical and musical criticisms of George Bernard Shaw. These are works of art in themselves, and will help place the sometimes fatuous and often self-involved critiques of your work in perspective. The most illuminating critique I've ever had came during a piece on an improvisational band I performed with. "If I knew what bar Larry Kirwan currently drinks in, I'd go there, toss back eight pints of Guinness, thrust my fingers down my throat, and throw up all over him." Now, that's what I call pointed and revealing criticism. It's colorful, active, lays it on the line, and, most important, gets to the point in one sentence.

Why would anyone wish to be an artist? you might ask. In my case, there was no plan—I backed into it by accident and general carelessness. I was definitely looking for adventure when I came to New York. Music, at that time, was at the cutting edge of society, and that's where I wanted to be: in the thick of the excitement. Besides, you didn't have to get up early in the morning, and there was always the off chance that you'd get laid. Times have changed, rock music is ubiquitous and about as relevant as a toilet-paper advertisement, and when was the last time a play or book caused a political or social stir? And yet we rock and write and read on! Perhaps it's because when you're creating, you get a heightened sense of yourself. As a musician friend once put it, "It's like you're living life at double speed."

Of course, you may be going nowhere in a hurry or racing off down some road to ruin. But you're never bored, and life is always more than it appears to be. And that's not a bad thing.

# Eugene O'Neill

*(October 16, 1888–November 27, 1953)*

American Drama was born on the night of July 28, 1916, in a little theater on a wharf in the sea town of Provincetown, Massachusetts. It was there that a twenty-seven-year-old Eugene O'Neill witnessed the staging of his first play, *Bound East for Cardiff*. The play, about the death of a sailor onboard a ship, could not have found a more apt home. The crusty old wharf reeked of fish oil and rubber boots, the floorboards creaked as the waves lapped against the pylons under the feet of the rapt audience, and in the distance the mournful wail of a foghorn could be heard from across the harbor. It was as if the universe conspired to bring O'Neill's voice and his introduction of psychological realism to the stage. Theater would never again be the same.

O'Neill himself was born in New York City, in a hotel room on Broadway and Forty-third street on October 16 ,1888. The details surrounding his birth and his parents' relationship are important to note because they would haunt the tone of O'Neill's work for his entire career.

Eugene's father, James, was a well known stage actor of his time. James was Irish-born, to a farmer in Kilkenny at the tail end of the famine. Eugene's mother, Ella, was the daughter of well-to-do Irish immigrants, Bridget and Thomas Quinlin from Tipperary. Ella might have been as young as fourteen when she first met the dapper James, who was eleven years her senior and already quite famous, when he visited her father's house in Cleveland, Ohio. It's easy to understand how she might have been smitten from the outset by the sight of the dashing young thespian with the hint of a brogue.

James was not exactly the kind of suitor Ella's parents had hoped for. Her mother tried to warn her about the perils of marrying an actor who toured constantly. Ella would not be swayed.

For Ella, it was to be a life of hotel rooms and tending to her children alone while James performed and socialized into the wee hours from city to city. She did the best she could to maintain order and to impart her own pious Irish Catholic upbringing to her children. The struggle with God and religion also would inform O'Neill's work his entire career.

Tragedy struck the O'Neills in the winter of 1885, when Ella left her first two children with her mother in New York while she went off to join her husband, James, on the road in Denver. While she was gone, James Jr. contracted measles. He passed it along to his younger brother, Edmund. Edmund died before Ella could make it back to see him. Ella was devastated, and in her grief blamed Edmund for passing the measles along to his younger brother. She vowed never to have another child. Two years later she was pregnant with Eugene.

It was the details around Eugene's birth in that hotel room that had the most profound effect on the tone of his writing.

James O'Neill was rumored to have been a tightfisted man. When Eugene was born, James sent a doctor he'd met in a bar to attend to his wife. She was in immense pain following the birth of Eugene, and it was this doctor who first prescribed her morphine. Given the physical pain of childbirth combined with the grief she still felt at the loss of Edmund and the loneliness she had to contend with due to an absentee husband, the morphine must have granted her immeasurable relief. Ella developed an immediate dependency on the drug that would last for practically the rest of her life. When he was a teenager, Eugene walked in on his mother injecting herself with the drug. It was a sight that would haunt him forever.

Later in life, O'Neill would voice his discontent with the uncertainty of a childhood spent in such disarray. He was a boy raised with practically no emotional sustenance. He spent the first seven years of his life in hotel rooms with a morphine-addicted mother, following his father's theater company from one city to the next, before being shipped off to Saint Aloysius Academy for boys in Riverdale, the Bronx, where he received a strict Catholic upbringing.

He attended Princeton briefly between 1906 and 1907, but he was a restless and reckless young man, choosing instead to travel. He spent several years at sea, drinking heavily. He was on a mission to get as far away from his upbringing as possible.

Between 1912 and 1913, he was hospitalized in a sanitarium for tuberculosis. It was during this time that he began to soberly take stock of the path he was on, and to write plays for the first time. For the next few years, he burrowed his way into his work. He wrote about what he knew best—drinking, derelicts, prostitutes, God, and sailors. He returned to study for a year at Harvard and in 1916 he joined the Provincetown Players on Cape Cod, where he started knocking out a series of short one-act plays, watching how they were produced, refining his craft in the buildup to his first real full-length play, *Beyond the Horizon*, for which he won his first Pulitzer Prize in 1920.

O'Neill was awarded the Pulitzer Prize another three times, for *Anna Christie, Strange Interlude,* and *Long Day's Journey into Night.*. The others were awarded for *Anna Christie, Strange Interlude,* and *Long Day's Journey into Night.* For the next twenty years, his reputation grew steadily, both in the United States and abroad; after Shakespeare and Shaw, O'Neill became the most widely translated and produced dramatist the world has ever known.

In 1936 Eugene O'Neill became the first American playwright to receive the Nobel Prize for literature. After winning the prize, he withdrew further and further from public life, becoming more and more reclusive and saving his energy only for his work.

On November 27, 1953, in room 401 of the Sheraton Hotel on Bay State Road, Boston, as Eugene O'Neill lay dying, he whispered his infamous last words: "I knew it. I knew it. Born in a hotel room—and God damn it—died in a hotel room."

Colin Broderick

# Kathleen Donohoe

Kathleen Donohoe was raised in Brooklyn, in a family of New York City firefighters. Her stories and essays have appeared in *The Recorder: The Journal of the American Irish Historical Society, New York Stories, Web Conjunctions, Washington Square Review, Irish America* magazine. Her debut novel, *Ashes of Fiery Weather,* was published in 2016. She currently lives in Brooklyn with her husband and son and is at work on her next novel.

# Brooklyn, Writer

## Heights

When I moved back to Brooklyn, the first apartment I looked at was on Montague Terrace. It was a five-floor walkup with one window, a kitchen sink, a refrigerator, but no oven. A studio, technically, though *attic* would have been more accurate. Montague Terrace is a small street dark with shade. The rent was $900.

The first time I read that writers were "flocking" to Park Slope, probably in the late nineties,

I laughed. Park Slope? Where Grandma and Pop-Pop lived? I'd grown up in Midwood. Being from Brooklyn meant little more than amusement in the face of almost universal surprise. But you don't have an accent! So where in Ireland were you born? Avenue J, I'd answer. At least twice I've gotten, "Kathleen Donohoe from Brooklyn? Are your father and uncles all cops or all they all firemen?" Firemen.

But before long, that's what writers did. They moved to Brooklyn, and not just for cheaper rent than Manhattan. It was a thing: Brooklyn Writer. Every time I heard this, I felt proprietary, as though I'd found someone who looked just like me living in my childhood bedroom.

My parents had moved to Long Island when I was nineteen, and for years after college, I lived there, commuting to stultifying secretarial jobs in the city while trying to write a novel at night and on weekends. My second novel. The first one had not sold. Desperate for time to write, for the chance to make connections in publishing, I decided to get an MFA. My goal from the time I started grad school was to finish the coursework and then, in Brooklyn, finish my thesis. I'd never imagined lucking into Brooklyn Heights. I took the apartment without hesitating. It was July 2005 and I was thirty-three years old.

During my time on Montague Terrace, these things happened:

I worked as a receptionist in a midtown Manhattan staffing firm. Southampton College closed due to bankruptcy. I never did get the degree. Ten years after I started it, I finished writing my second novel. After five months of cold querying and sixty rejections, I signed with a literary agent.

I went on a blind date at a wine bar in the Village called the B*ourgeois* Pig. Normally, I would have recoiled at the idea of being set up, but the mutual friend who arranged it said, "He's really good-looking. I was really disappointed when I found out he was straight." Intrigued, I went. That was April. New Year's Eve 2007 Travis and I spent together. The year I sell a book.

I began to think seriously about the next book. I had two ideas. One book was quirky and quick. The other was, in part, about September 11th.

My family did not lose anyone, spared by luck and the era in which the attack occurred. My uncles had all retired by 2001. Neither my father nor my cousin were working that day, though my cousin had been on the night before, and we didn't confirm that he was alive until the early morning hours of September 12th. I began writing the other book. Quirky. Quick.

One day, spring of 2008, I checked my email before leaving work. My agent had written to tell me of a rejection. Going forward, he wrote, he would continue to submit the book as he heard of new possibilities. Outside, I stepped into midtown Manhattan's pedestrian rush hour. Waiting for the light at the corner of Fifty-third and Park Avenue, I wanted to sink to the curb.

My coworkers at the staffing firm had once given me a card on Administrative Professionals Day, and I did appreciate their thoughtfulness. I took the card home and set it on fire. Writer, I thought as I watched the card burn in the kitchen sink. I'm a writer. Somebody give me that card.

I didn't sit down. I crossed the street and caught the subway back to Brooklyn.

Travis left Cobble Hill and I left Brooklyn Heights and we moved into a one-bedroom apartment in Park Slope.

## Brownstone

In January 2010, Travis and I moved to Carroll Gardens.

The year before, in Park Slope, we had gone most of the winter without heat or hot water.

The landlord had more excuses than fingers as to why the furnace could not be fixed. Our theory? That he might be trying to freeze out his rent-controlled tenants. When the lease was up, we left, though we'd spent close to $5,000 to move in only the year before. Some of our experiences were more Park Slope–typical, though, like going to the Greenmarket at Grand Army Plaza, jogging in Prospect Park, getting pregnant.

In Carroll Gardens, we lived on the third floor of a brownstone, in a one-bedroom-plus-den. The stoop was ours. Two weeks after we moved in, Travis and I got married in Brooklyn's City Hall. Seventeen days after the wedding, our son was born. After my maternity leave was up, Liam went into a daycare that cost more than our rent. With husband and son added to my health insurance, my paycheck dropped to $300 a week. I joined the Brooklyn Writers Space on Court Street in Cobble Hill, which gave me a place to write outside of our four-room apartment. I went there on Saturday and Sunday mornings, hoping to finish my (third) novel before maxing out my credit card.

Once Liam was sleeping (sort of) regularly, Travis and I would get up at 5:00 a.m., me to write before work and Travis to edit audio books for his part-time freelance job. During the day, he edited audio books for a different company, a full-time job, but freelance as well.

After Liam was born, we were often asked if we now planned

to leave Brooklyn. We did not want to, but wondered if we should. As much as we loved Carroll Gardens, we were only there because our apartment was a steal. Certainly, we were luckier than many; as a freelancer, Travis was often underemployed during the recession, but never entirely unemployed. As the receptionist at the staffing firm, my position singular, I escaped each round of layoffs. Yet we listened to casual conversations in Carroll Park about where to buy a house and when to have the second baby. Travis's salary fluctuated from month to month. Often, I would have less than twenty dollars in my account by payday.

Travis would say, "You need to finish that book and sell it."

I would laugh and explain—again—that the average advance for an unknown first-time novelist was about $25,000. Buy a lottery ticket.

Stowaways in gentrified Brooklyn, we were constantly searching for better work, a better way to be.

## Garden

Shortly before Liam's first birthday, I came home from a job interview at Brooklyn Botanic Garden, an administrative position in the offices, and said that if I got it, I would never publish a novel because I would have used up my allotment of luck for this lifetime. The salary was lower, but so was the cost of health insurance. More than enough to compensate.

After I began working at the Garden, the thought returned when I was particularly despairing of finishing the book, or when we weren't sure if we'd have the rent. The new job helped, but student loan debt (both of us), twelve weeks' unpaid maternity leave, and a year of paying $1,000 a month for insurance could not be easily undone. Still, I refused to give up Brooklyn Writers Space, too bothered by noise to take a chance on the library or a coffee shop.

A bold gamble, foolishness, or plain denial.

Stepping out onto blooming Magnolia Plaza. Going out of my way while heading home just to pass by Bluebell Wood. Sitting with Liam by the tulips after hours, the Garden quiet, I was almost accepting. Here you go. Here is the consolation prize for the dream that will never come true.

## Exit

On my fortieth birthday, October 27, 2012, I finished writing my third novel. The first draft was more than six hundred pages. It had taken three years to write. Months earlier, I'd officially severed ties with my former agent, a technicality, since we had not been in touch for years.

I searched agentquery.com and spent every lunch hour in the library at Grand Army Plaza, where I would slip book after book off its shelf and, with one deft movement that was all in the wrist, flip it over and open it backwards. If the agent was thanked in the acknowledgments, I jotted down the name in my notebook.

For months, I scored requests for the manuscript without getting to yes. I borrowed money from my mother so I could go to a writers' conference in Manhattan, where I pitched the novel to five agents and one editor. All six asked to see the manuscript. By June, all six had passed. I gave up Brooklyn Writers Space.

One July night, sick with bronchitis worthy of winter, I went online to check for rejections, which came at all hours as though I were querying agents in every time zone. It was about 9:30 p.m. I had an email from an agent who'd had the full manuscript since May. I read the line that was visible.

*Sorry to take so long to get back to you but*

"Not tonight," I said out loud. I only wanted to collapse in bed. I clicked.

*I've finished the novel and think there is a lot of potential here.*

On August 3, 2013, after seven months of querying and seventy-five rejections, I signed with an agent whose name I'd culled from the acknowledgments of a novel I'd loved.

Two weeks later, our landlady informed us that she was selling the house. The brownstone went on the market a month later and sold in fifteen minutes for more than the asking price. About $2 million. Though our lease wasn't up until January, we agreed to leave on the Friday after Thanksgiving. There was no reason to prolong it.

## Sweet

By January 2014, we'd been living at my parents' house for three months, commuting on the Long Island Railroad during one of the most brutal winters in recent memory, and apartment-hunting on the weekends. The day we left Brooklyn, I'd gotten the edits for my novel from my agent, so I was revising it after work and before catching a train back to Long Island. Two landlords rejected our applications after the credit check. Several brokers would not even show us the places we'd called about. Your combined income isn't high enough. It's too small for three people. This landlord doesn't accept guarantors.

Travis quit his jobs to do nothing but look for full-time, permanent work. A complete career switch to the tech industry was the only way to solvency. He'd been making inroads for some time. Now, while we were not paying rent, was the time to go for it.

It took a month. Travis's first day at his new job in the Flatiron District (Quality Assurance Engineer) was February 18th. On February 21st, my novel went out to editors. On February 22nd, Liam turned four.

A week later, based on Travis's new salary, and with my father as guarantor, we found an apartment in Kensington, a neighborhood in between Prospect Park and the Green-Wood Cemetery. Instead of sober brownstones, Kensington's blocks are lined with redbrick row houses and wood-frame houses sided in blue or green or red. We took over the lease on March 15th.

But let's go back five days.

On March 10th, I spent the morning at work, waiting to hear from my agent. An editor from Houghton Mifflin Harcourt loved my novel and wanted to acquire it, but first had to pitch it to her colleagues at an acquisitions meeting. Around noon, my agent emailed to tell me we had an offer and to call her. Let it be at least $25,000, I thought as I dialed.

I still wonder what I would have said, when I heard the number, had I been able to speak. Before I could make an attempt, my agent added that she'd told the editor it was not enough, and now we'd wait and see what they came back with.

At 4:00 p.m., I left work and was walking up Washington Avenue beside the black iron gate that surrounds Brooklyn Botanic Garden. The phone rang. Your novel has sold. This one, and the next one, yet to be written. A two-book deal, not for quit-your-job-this-second money, unless you're a fool, but far more than I'd ever let myself imagine as a real possibility. I was, from one moment to the next, debt free. Given the chance to start over, to get it right. My name would be spelled out on the spine of a book. The book would be on the shelf of the library at Grand Army Plaza, in between Emma Donoghue and Keith Donohue.

It was a good Saint Patrick's Day.

## Bridge

Even given all that happened when I lived in Brooklyn Heights, when I look back on that time, I think first of running. Every night after work, I jogged the length of the promenade and emerged at the Fruit Street Sitting Area on Columbia Heights. I ran past the firehouse on Middagh Street with the September 11th mural painted on its door. Cadman Park came next.

Once a rat slammed into my sneaker. We stopped short, two horrified New Yorkers who had accidentally touched. I shuddered, it probably did too, and then we both ran on. Under the overpass, up the narrow stairwell, and I was on the Brooklyn Bridge. Nights, I often had it to myself. Every evening, I ran towards the city. Without the towers, Manhattan looked like a person whose eyes have simply vanished.

The bridge is said to be haunted. Men died while building it. A woman, the wife of one of them, purportedly used it to leap to her death. In 1883, the weekend after it opened, twelve people were crushed in a stampede caused by a rumor that the bridge was about to collapse.

I thought, too, of the living who'd fled Manhattan on a beautiful Tuesday morning turned to ash.

Three hundred and forty-three firefighters were killed. One hundred and forty-six were members of the FDNY's Emerald Society. One third of all first responders killed either lived or worked in Brooklyn. In Googling the number of Brooklynites who died, I've found "over 300" and "about 270."

Quirky. Quick. I set that book aside. Once I had become the author of two unsold novels, "audience" returned to abstraction. I was again alone with my writing. And when you're talking to yourself, you're free to say whatever you want. I saw that I'd been afraid of the FDNY book, both for its scope and its subject. When I thought of the story, I could not sense its edges; being from a fire family myself, wasn't it worse than if an outsider co-opted and fictionalized that grief? Yet as the book became itself, that is, more than an idea and a scatter of notes, I began to believe that it would not be a betrayal. Not if I did it well. To put it in Brooklynese:

Write the book. Don't fuck it up.

How to not fuck it up?

On September 11th, after almost a half hour of trying, I'd

73

reached my mother by phone. She and my father had been at the dentist. There had been a recall, she said. Every firefighter in the city had to report for duty.

"Your father had to go to work."

That was it. Stand on that sentence, bare of mythology, sentiment, or sanctimony. Stand on that sentence and write the book from there.

*The Ashes of Fiery Weather* was set to be published in the fall of 2015. The novel

is about the women of a Brooklyn family of firefighters whose stories interconnect across generations, from famine-era Ireland to ten years after September 11th.

I never did seek out Brooklyn's vibrant literary community. In my attic on Montague Terrace, I had often searched online for local readings, book signings, and literary parties. I should, I told myself, meet people. Network! But if an event was on a weekend, I watched the clock tick past the time I'd planned to leave. If it was after work, I went home and went running instead.

Brooklyn is full of brilliant writers who have moved here to do their work, to find a community. I came to realize that I can never quite be one of them. I didn't come to Brooklyn to find my voice. It is my voice.

Every night for three years, I would touch the toes of my sneakers to the line where Brooklyn becomes Manhattan, and turn back. I have never seen a ghost up there. Is the bridge haunted? I don't know. This is what I know:

If Brooklyn is the Borough of Churches, then the bridge is its cathedral. The bridge is most beautiful at dusk. The bridge cannot save everyone. The bridge will always be the way home.

"I began to like New York, the racy, adventurous feel of it at night and the satisfaction that the constant flicker of men and women and machines gives to the restless eye. I like to walk up Fifth Avenue and pick out romantic women from the crowd and imagine that in a few minutes I was going to enter their lives, and no one would ever know or disapprove. Sometimes, in my mind, I followed them to their apartments on the corners of hidden streets, and they turned and smiled back at me before they faded through a door into warm darkness. At the enchanted metropolitan twilight I felt a haunting loneliness sometimes, and felt it in others—poor young clerks who loitered in front of windows waiting until it was time for a solitary restaurant dinner—young clerks in the dusk, wasting the most poignant moments of night and life."

*The Great Gatsby*

# *F. Scott Fitzgerald*

*(September 24, 1896–December 21, 1940)*

# Daniel James McCabe

Daniel James McCabe was born in Queens, New York, to a massive Irish-American family who instilled in him a deep love of storytelling, music, and cinema. He is the founder of *Glasschord* magazine and the winner of the Award for Excellence in Playwriting at the 2014 International Fringe Festival. His play *The Flood* premiered in Belfast's Lyric Theatre in 2014. He lives in Brooklyn with his wife and two children.

# The Poet's Paradox

In *Hamlet,* Shakespeare has the prince proclaim that as artists we hold up a mirror to nature. Four centuries later, in *Ulysses,* Joyce feeds his proxy Stephen a metaphor more specific to his own milieu. The young man holds a broken mirror and says, "It is a symbol of Irish art. The cracked looking-glass of a servant."

The most worthy art, in my opinion, is that in which the artist displays courage enough to show the world to itself, beautiful and cruel and noble and self-destructive as it is. Of course this is impossible. First of all, the world does not want to see itself as it is. It wants not constructive criticism but careless corroboration, and it will go to great lengths in its desire to distort its own image. Second, as writers, filmmakers, painters . . . as artists, we all bring our individual perspective, our experience, our own empirical knowledge to the endeavor. No matter how one tries to present an unbiased and "truthful" work, there is always the world-wrought mind from which it grew, and another artist might cast the same subject in dramatically different light. All one can do is be honest, and by *honest* I mean steadfast and committed to the fidelity of one's own earnest impressions. It is only by doing so that a meaningful reflection can be made, and we can penetrate beyond the surfaces of things to understand them, and one another, better. Just as the facets of a cracked looking glass reflect varying, sometimes paradoxical angles, so do we. And if there is a place to search for the essence of art's redeeming power to unify, to begin the endeavor to understand one another, it is in the cracks between our reflections of the world.

\*\*\*

While most of the contributors to this collection will likely be full-blooded children of Erin, I confess from the start that I'm an

Irish-New York alloy. I was born in Queens, statistically the most culturally diverse urban area in the world, so as circumstances would have it I was raised not only by my paternal Irish family but also by my maternal Australian and Sicilian family. In effect I am seventy-five percent brooding Gael and a quarter hot-blooded Latin, which is just enough to make me a double agent in the war with myself.

My father, whose family has been in New York for more than a century and a half, is one of fourteen children, twelve of whom survived to adulthood. When we lost my grandmother Audrey Catherine, matriarch of the McCabe tribe, the tally of her living children, grandchildren, and great-grandchildren was eighty-seven. All of them unique, all of them able and most of them willing to argue fiercely for their own point of view. So while I am a New Yorker of mixed ancestry, the dominant cultural voice of my childhood was unmistakably Irish, and it was from my Irish family that the mad notion to pursue a life telling stories came.

My first ancestors to leave Ireland did so with death at their heels and arrived in Manhattan around 1847, a year before the *Times* of London's sadistic boast that "a Celt will soon be as rare on the banks of the Shannon as the red man on the banks of Manhattan." We arrived in a city deeply hostile to the flood of Irish Catholics pouring in. The anti-immigrant and absurdly named "Nativists," many of whom had only been in the New World for a generation, had the idea that New York was for them alone. They had long since made this idea manifest on the Canarsie, the Rockaway, the Lenape—the true native inhabitants of Mannahatta and Paumanok.

Jobs were scarce for most immigrants and scarcer for the Irish. In hiring for what lowly jobs there were, the employers made their prejudice plain in the now infamous "No Irish Need Apply" signs hung outside their shops. Our first ancestors in

New York survived by taking the most menial and dangerous work available, forced into competition not only with their own but also with Africans, both slave and free, the ethnic group in the city with whom they had the most in common.

Members of my early New York family moved through the Five Points and into the Lower East Side, some soon leaving New York to fight and die for the Union in the American Civil War. By the early years of the twentieth century, some had spread across the river into Williamsburg, where my great-grandfather, "One Eyed Mike" McCabe, opened a bar and continued to operate it through Prohibition. From Williamsburg the family went to the old Ninth Ward near Ebbets Field, Bedford-Stuyvesant, Marine Park, South Queens. My daughter, Tierney Rose, who was born in Manhattan, is an eighth-generation New Yorker. Her accent belongs to her age, but she understands that cars need occasional *erl* changes, that she has *coyly* hair, and that in our family it's best to cut straight to the *pernt*.

My grandfather Francis Michael McCabe, who passed away when I was three, remains a mythic figure in my mind. I have vague memories of his company, and of the nervous hush through his final days at home, where he wanted to die if he had to die at all. I know that one sunny day not long before his passing my father brought me to see him. My grandfather took me up onto his lap while my father stepped out to collect my grandmother and maybe pick up a beef-tongue sandwich and a celery soda for Grandpa. He sang to me, held me up, and nuzzled me against the stubble on his chin to my giggling delight until eventually I got away from him. There was a tall Norwegian spruce in the small front yard, and beneath it was always shady and cool and there was a soft bed of fallen pine needles to play in. Evidently that's where I went. When my father returned from his errand, he saw me under the tree and my grandfather crawling down the front steps on his elbows, reaching out blindly and calling my name. His sickness had taken his sight by then, along with both of his legs.

As a younger man, he'd been a dynamo. He was a longshoreman, a steelworker, a cabdriver, a bartender, a singing waiter in Coney Island. My grandmother managed the home and the brood of children and worked part-time at the rectory at Saint Teresa's, their parish in Queens. They never bought new things for themselves but mended what they had and made it last. The children, meanwhile, lived on an endless cycle of hand-me-down clothing, books, records, ideas. They grew up tough and fast and bursting with life. It's no wonder I was drawn to writing, as the people who raised me are each in their own distinct way characters of such complexity, humor, and explosive enthusiasm that as a boy I couldn't help but attempt to describe them to myself.

They had not neglected history. They maintained a tradition of Irish Republicanism very often forgotten by other immigrant Irish who wore their new American identities with anonymous relief, trading their sense of sedition for a place at the table. I was educated in America, a country my forebears deeply loved as the place where they found freedom in a society that would, eventually, allow them to be more than mere peasants, but I was taught always to read between the lines and never accept at face value the things people in power would have me believe.

Like that of most Celts, our early family history was not written down but passed along orally, and if ever it was compiled, the documents remain lost to the desperate flight from what most historians have termed a "famine." This tradition of storytelling and narrative music survived throughout my childhood, and I can remember long family parties in our backyard in Queens, wailing pipes, high voices, and the rhythmic thrum of the bodhran late into the night. Outside the home, a different world waited, one I didn't yet know as well as I did the world of our family, and it whispered to me promises of stories and songs I could make for my own. It had to. My uncles had been street kids in the New York of the sixties and seventies. They had chased girls, fought rivals, found allies, collided with the other cultures of our motley city. My father had been a bartender, a voracious reader, and a promising heavyweight in the Golden Gloves until I came along and he began a long and storied career with the NYPD. He rose quickly from a short stint in uniform to eventually become the commanding officer of the Manhattan South homicide squad. He did his job well. It is not something commonly understood these days, but as a means of providing context to those that lack it, I'll say that in 1990, when I was eleven years old and wandering the streets of Queens, there were more than 2,200 homicides in New York. Last year, in 2014, there were 328.

I spent most of the fourth grade in the back of the classroom writing an adventure novel. Three kids from the neighborhood find a magical trunk in an attic and discover it's a time portal that sends them back to Arthurian England to aid Merlin and the king in their battle against Mordred, who I envisioned as a street punk in black chain mail. At home I read everything I was given, and when I thirsted for more, I wore my library card out. My father took pride in his own library, and I gorged my imagination on his atlases, encyclopedias, and a beautifully illustrated astronomy book that profiled each of the deities ascribed to the planets and stars. I loved Dixon's detective novels, and when I was eight attempted a Hardy Boys-style book of my own. Inspired by the movie *The Neverending Story,* I insisted upon reading all of Tolkien by candlelight, which I thought might pull me further into the pages and my mother was sure would leave me blind.

I fell in love with cinema, which blended all art forms but began with my favorite, the birth of a story on paper. When

I was lucky, my parents would buy me cassette tapes of the soundtracks to my favorite films, soaring scores by Danny Elfman, John Williams, and Alan Silvestri, which I would listen to through headphones as my pen flew across the pages. It was pure joy to write as a child, to hurl myself into it with unbridled and unselfconscious abandon. I found so much freedom in the act of writing that I knew it was what I wanted to do, not once I'd grown up but until then, and for the rest of my life.

Then, at some point around my twelfth birthday, I discovered Yeats. Everything changed. I felt a strange connection to the imagery, the mystical stone figures shrouded in smoke, the pastoral longing and brooding gravitas. I had come to know many of the biblical references Yeats conjured and some of the classical mythology, but knew little of the pagan symbolism or history he evoked, and it drew me in with its mystery. The arrival of Yeats revealed a profound and powerful aspect to the writer's task that as a boy I had not yet considered. Here was not reckless scribbling for the mere joy of it but intense, laborious effort in pursuit of deep universal truth. It made the craft of verse all the more alluring. I took my notebooks everywhere I went and filled them day by day.

In my fourteenth summer, I went to work at an oceanfront bar called Chauncey's in Long Beach, New York. My uncle Terry had been a manager there, and I worked as a barback, busboy, and service bartender through high school. If there is in the world a way to peer behind the masks of maturity and into the intricate and half-mad human soul, it is as a sober boy obliged by duty to serve in a sea of drunken adults. Most of the time I went unnoticed by the crowd, as though wearing Tolkien's magic ring, and it made my observations all the more authentic. I saw romance, heartbreak, euphoric camaraderie, and explosive violence. Alliances were made and shattered, clandestine rendezvous consummated, and some people simply broken. I remember the sad-eyed bathroom attendant perched at the end of the bar in the mornings as I stocked the liquor, a woman of nearly seventy years and in her off-hours filled with vodka and fantasies of leaving, of finding her son, of beginning again. And at the end of each shift, the crashing waves waited for me just steps from the back door, where I would sit on the sand and scribble my ceaseless fascination with the uninhibited displays of the people I'd found in this strange new world.

Then, when I was sixteen, we opened a bar of our own. It was situated in the middle of the block on Lexington Avenue between Twenty-eighth and Twenty-ninth streets, an Irish bar in the heart of Little India. We called it Rocky Sullivan's, after Jimmy Cagney's character in *Angels with Dirty Faces*. I worked behind the bar, the legality of which was often pondered by the clientele. It was there that I first met Pete Hamill, Jimmy Breslin, Frank and Malachy McCourt, and shaking their hands I got the sense that professional writing was actually something that could be done by people who came from the kinds of places I did. There were lesser known artists as well, among them a guitar-playing boxer called Damien Dempsey and a young and quick-witted scribe named Colum McCann. I was given my first book of poems by Seamus Heaney, and another by Paul Muldoon. Martin McGuinness gave me a volume of Patrick Kavanagh's work and I read from it to the crowd at one of our frequent literary events. One night Shane MacGowan came in and I served him pints of gin on the rocks for five hours and never once did he get up from his seat. At about 6:00 a.m. he thanked me with a rendition of "Danny Boy," the most horrific I've heard in my life.

The clientele at Rocky's was more diverse than Chauncey's, both socially and culturally. Construction workers rubbed elbows with NYU professors, communists with Wall Street traders, local politicians with lunatic Scottish football fans. The cracks in the mirror seemed more plentiful than ever, and in the unlikely convergences of such a disparate assembly, the beauty of the New York experiment dazzled me, and through it all I listened, and wrote.

I've had the privilege of traveling to Ireland a fair bit throughout my life. As a boy my father's affiliation with Sinn Fein brought us more often to the North than the Republic, though regardless of which side of the border I was on, I always learned a great deal from my hosts. In Belfast and Derry I experienced the reality of state-sponsored racism, and it deepened my sympathy for victims of oppression everywhere. I also was invited to partake in the beautiful bond that is forged by such conditions. The mirth, musicality, and solidarity so widely accepted as the Irish character that it's now cliché did not come without a tremendous cost. Every time I returned to New York, I did so with an enhanced perspective, and my journeys to Ireland have tempered my outlook ever since. Home in New York I'd always found distasteful the ostensible Irishness of goons swilling green beer and jumping to House of Pain on Saint Patrick's Day, but after each successive trip to Ireland, I found my embarrassment of such empty displays had deepened exponentially.

By twenty I was writing more than I ever had, and read with a greater appetite than before. I'd moved on to Joyce, Salinger, Hesse, the Beats, Whitman, Emerson, Hemingway, Eliot, and Cummings and the poets of the Harlem Renaissance. Eventually I stopped working at Rocky's, which was consuming far too much of my strength, and got a job at a photo studio in SoHo, where I spent nearly ten years. I went to Ireland on my own for a couple of months and wrote a film script in the Dublin home of a dear woman called Clare Barry, who was leaving for New York and decided I should stay there in her absence. Clare made this decision after meeting me at a dinner party only once, and when I offered, she refused payment of any kind.

Someone once told me you're not a real Irish writer from New York unless you have a union card in your pocket, and I don't think he was referring to the WGA, so along the way I joined Local 52, the studio mechanic's union. The film industry in New York was being steadily reinvigorated, and I snuck in to find myself a place on set. The hours are murder but the pay is good, and I've met so many brilliant, gifted, and beguilingly insane people that I've developed an almost addictive fixation with the life. It's an agony when I'm in it, and I miss it sorely when I'm not. I've been blessed to run with an excellent crew, one of the best in the city, and comprised of some of my dearest friends. I'll jump on a film, which usually takes about three months to shoot, then cut out for a month or two to cloister myself off in the studio and write.

Movie folk are an arcane subculture made up of artisans, virtuosos, raconteurs, and roustabouts, and in the chaotic confluence of a film set one moves freely and routinely between each. The filmmaking community is another fine example of the enchanting variety of perspectives available to anyone willing to look for them, another paradoxical place between the plates of nature's fractured reflections, where the tangible work of laconic laborers dovetails with the visions of the world's most exuberant storytellers, many of whom are reaching for real art.

In 2012 I had a regular gig on an ill-fated series for ABC. When Hurricane Sandy hit in October, the show suffered such damages that it was required to halt production for a week. I lost my grandmother Yvonne the night of the storm and sat down the following evening to write her a eulogy. When I'd finished her tribute, I still had more to say. By the time shooting resumed on my job, I'd completed the first draft of a play that would eventually be called *The Flood*.

I knew nothing of the workings of the theater world, but I did know that eventually I'd need to hear the script read aloud. That meant actors, and I needed four. In my naivete, I figured that I would do for one of them, and my wife, Emma Ishta, who today is the star of a TV show, had just taken her first steps into acting as a profession, so there were two. An actress from the series I was working on suggested a friend of hers, a beautiful uptown girl with a kind and gentle manner. We needed one more man to play the part of a tender tough guy from Derry, and a friend in the arts suggested John Duddy.

Anyone who's even had a peek into Irish culture over the past fifteen years is likely to have heard of John. As a champion middleweight boxer, he made headlines, preceded everywhere by his reputation as a gentleman. Irish New York loved him, especially after his legendary series of fights at Madison Square Garden. I'd heard he'd been stepping into acting since his retirement from the fight game, and we had a few friends in common, so it was arranged that we'd meet and discuss the part. On Sunday, February 3rd, 2013, I printed a copy of the script and went up to meet him at a joint on Fifty-seventh street. When I walked in, I spotted him standing at the far end of the bar in a white shirt and black tie. I approached quietly and held a large brown paper envelope out to him.

"You Daniel?" he asked, a little bit on guard.

I nodded. "Nice to meet you J—"

"—Ye look like fookin' Orson Welles!" he said to me, which isn't the worst thing to hear if you're trying to get a play on its feet. I did wonder whether he meant *Citizen Kane*-era Welles or *Catch-22* era Welles, but I figured it best just to take it as a compliment. We went downtown together and then later out to Queens, spent hours talking, laughing, and singing, and without quite knowing it yet, I made one of the closest allies I've ever had.

So we put a reading together at a friend's loft in SoHo. About fifty people attended, and the response was encouraging. From there, Chris Cahill of the American-Irish Historical Society was kind enough to host us twice, and each time the feedback got more interesting and the story more refined. Jane McCarter of the New York Irish Center invited us out for another reading, and then on Terry George's recommendation, Ciaran O'Reilly offered us a place in the renowned Irish Repertory Theatre's reading series. My old friend Colum McCann attended, now an internationally acclaimed novelist, along with many others, most of whom were complete strangers to me.

Shortly after that, *The Flood* was selected for the 2014 New York International Fringe Festival. We led an incredibly generous fundraising campaign to cover production costs, and I stumbled blindly into the rehearsal process, directing and producing while preparing to act in our run of five shows. Tickets went on sale on a Monday, and by Friday morning we were sold out, the first of more than two hundred festival companies to do so. In response, the Fringe added a show and it sold out in about forty minutes. It was a trial by fire, one I would most certainly have burned up in if not for the support and talents of my wife, Emma, and of the cast and crew we'd managed to assemble.

I learned a great deal through that time, and I'm grateful to everyone who gave us the chance to hold our cracked looking-glass to the world. In the end, once the stage had been swept and the rentals returned, I found that *The Flood* had been given the New York Fringe Festival's award for Excellence in Playwriting.

\*\*\*

These days I write more than ever. When it happens that I'm short of inspiration, I walk the streets of the city I love. These are the same streets my forefathers walked, the earliest of whom had been among the city's despised. Their ghosts, and the ghosts of countless others, roam these streets with all of us. "Remember," they whisper, in a place prone to forgetting, where the only constant since its foundation has been the ceaseless tide of change, the transition of neighborhoods, attitudes, the collision and assimilation of clashing cultures and seemingly irreconcilable ideas. And through it all the city survives because it's built upon stronger foundations than the bedrock beneath Midtown or the Battery. It is built on the idea that people from every conceivable background or persuasion can find their humanity in common, and prosper together, and it has shown the world that this idea is provable and true. While this was not at all the purpose for which the city was founded, it's most certainly the means by which it has thrived.

The city, and the world, is constantly beset by those who would divide us, whose fearful and superficial efforts serve only to belabor our differences. But the city, and the world, will survive these fools. There are too many out there who are more concerned with that which unites us, who venture beyond their separate impressions and into the cracks between, the ones who know how to see one another and who understand the necessity, for our very survival, of our coexistence. That I should so often be blessed to encounter them as together we walk through these streets, that we should share a silent, anonymous smile of understanding, gives me all the inspiration I need to keep writing.

# Jimmy Breslin

*(October 17, 1928–March 19, 2017)*

By his own account, Jimmy Breslin is the grandfather of the scrappy, old-school, New York Irish street reporter. It's a claim hard to dispute. In the early days of New York newspapers, Breslin learned that a good reporter with his ear to the ground could get most of his news over drinks with ruddy-faced cops and sharply dressed crooks in dimly lit bars in the old Irish neighborhoods of Queens and the Bronx and the Upper East Side. If there was a whisper of a story, you could be sure Breslin heard it first.

The legend of Breslin spawned an army of copycat reporters all over town. If you were in the business of reporting the news, you hired a scrappy Irish street reporter—it was that simple. So what if he only ever showed up half sozzled after dark to frantically type a few lines of copy? Odds are the lonely clatter of those Remington keys in an empty newsroom were the best lines of copy you were going to read all day.

Breslin's main source of news was an Irish watering hole called Pep McGuire's out on Queens Boulevard. Pep McGuire's was the most notorious bar in the borough. Gangsters and cops drank side by side, made men sat next to undercover Feds. It was the local drinking spot for Jimmy Burke, the mastermind of the JFK Lufthansa heist, made famous in the movie *Goodfellas*. (Burke had Breslin attacked and viciously beaten for a piece he wrote about the Lucchese crime family. Breslin suffered a concussion and narrowly escaped permanent brain damage.) On any given day, you were as likely to see Breslin shoulder to shoulder at the stick with the chief of police as with mob boss John Gotti. Breslin was equally at home with both; as a child he'd been cruelly schooled in the harsher realities of the street.

He was born at the height of the Depression, October 17, 1928, in the working-class neighborhood of Jamaica, Queens. When he was about four, his father, a musician, went out on an errand and never returned. His mother, left to raise him by herself in Ozone Park, turned to the bottle. In his memoir *I Want to Thank my Brain for Remembering Me*, he recounts how as a boy he witnessed his mother hysterically drunk in their living room with a gun to her temple repeatedly pulling the trigger; the chamber, fortunately, happened to be empty. A few days later, he handwrote an account of what he'd witnessed, gave it the headline "Mother Tried Suicide," folded the piece of paper, and dropped it off at the local newsstand so they could sell it as copy. A reporter was born.

In his decades as a reporter, he drifted into some of the biggest stories of the century like some ink-smudged Zelig.

While in Washington, D.C., reporting on the death of John F. Kennedy, Breslin left the throngs of reporters at the morgue to visit Arlington Cemetery, where he struck up a conversation with a black man named Clifton Pollard who was digging the president's grave with a backhoe. The piece he wrote detailing Pollard's sense of civic duty, "It's an Honor," became one of the most valuable pieces of journalism ever written.

On June 5, 1968, in the lobby of the Ambassador Hotel in Los Angeles, Jimmy Breslin was present with fellow journalist Pete Hamill when Sirhan Sirhan shot and killed Robert F. Kennedy.

On the May 30, 1977, Breslin received a handwritten letter on his news desk from David Berkowitz, aka the Son of Sam, the serial killer who was still at large, terrorizing the streets of New York. "I'm just dropping you a line to let you know I appreciate your interest in those recent and horrendous .44 killings. I also want to tell you that I read your column and find it quite informative." After reading the letter, Breslin famously quipped; "The guy can write better than me." Breslin went on to play himself in the Spike Lee movie version of the story, *Summer of Sam*, in 1999.

In 1985, Jimmy Breslin was given the prestigious George Polk Award for Metropolitan Reporting. In 1986, he was awarded the Pulitzer Prize for commentary.

Rumor has it he is still at large.

Colin Broderick

# Mike Farragher

Mike Farragher wrote the music column for New York's premiere Irish news outlet, IrishCentral, for eighteen years. His first novel, *Collared,* was published in 2004. Since then he has published two humorous collections of essays, *This is Your Brain on Shamrocks,* and *This is Your Brain on Shamrocks 2.* His new book, *A Devilish Pint* was published in 2016. He is currently working on a his first play.

# The Collared One

Since we are known globally for our gift of storytelling, it stands to reason that every Irish person should have published at least one novel in his or her lifetime. As a race, we are a few billion books short of that reality.

Why?

If you're Irish and you've ever published a book, you have only done so by letting go of what it means to be Irish.

You've had to let go of the notion of keeping your head down and not appearing to "put on airs."

You've had to let go of the notion of not making too much of a spectacle of yourself.

You've had to let go of worrying what the neighbors think.

It took me thirty-seven years to let go of being Irish, and when I did, my first novel provoked a series of seismic shifts in my life that required me to open old wounds, pick the scabs, lather, rinse, repeat.

At the moment when I took a box cutter to the case of my first novel and held it in my hand, there was a swell of pride, as you can well imagine. For anyone who has been blessed with producing a child, the feeling of holding your baby in the delivery room is about the same.

There wasn't a lot of internal backslapping, though, as I recall—I was committed to letting go of a lot more than my Irishness that night, and my mind was focused on that. I took two copies of *Collared*, my novel of suspense set among the church sex scandals, and headed out the door to meet my parents for lunch.

"I've got good news and bad news," I announced once the waiter took our order.

"The good news is that you're not in the book."

"What book?" my father asked.

I slid the novel across the table. Their eyes focused on the name I shared with my dad that was etched underneath the gothic depiction of a white hand closing in on the throat of a silhouette with a priest's collar.

"You wrote this?" my mother asked, still trying to take it in. "What's it about?"

I told her the plotline of the book: Two brothers abused by a priest grow up and take two different paths. One becomes a priest while the other becomes a reporter who blows the lid off the church sex-abuse scandals. A killer targets the priest featured in the reporter's columns, and this leads the brothers to the priest who abused them for the explosive finale.

I could see the concern welling up in my mother, who has run the Rosary Society and the religious education programs in her parish for decades.

"This isn't something that trashes the church is it? What's it about?"

I told them the story behind the story.

A man who taught in my grammar school in my old neighborhood had entered into religious life, assumed the name Brother Dwight, and, in my sophomore year, joined the order that operated in my high school. Mom and Dad thought it was more of a coincidence; it was Divine Intervention! We had him over to the house, and little by little, he assumed the head seat at the table, especially when my dad was working double shifts on the New Jersey Turnpike.

Visiting priests, nuns, and religious brothers were treated like dignitaries, as is Irish custom. Their meals were served on the wedding china when everyone else ate their food on paper "chinette" plates.

"He sees something in you," my mother said proudly. For anyone with an Irish mother, a cleric who sees "something in you" meant there was clairvoyance to a vocation at play. When Brother Dwight suggested a weekend retreat up in the woods, my mother could not have packed the bags soon enough.

He saw something, all right. A fat, insecure kid whose father was away working crazy hours to keep afloat while the mother reverently poured her energy into her church was perfect prey for a man like Dwight.

There would always be a rich dinner that required a jacket and tie, followed by the dizzy thrill of sipping your first alcoholic beverage. On one trip to celebrate my sixteenth birthday, Dwight dressed in plain clothes and drove me to a special surprise. We soon found ourselves giggling nervously as we entered a topless doughnut shop. The waitresses served doughnuts with a sheer top and skimpy panties; I was transfixed by my first sight of a near-naked woman. When the right mixture of booze and visual stimuli would be at their peak, we would rush back to the room to "give the old man a workout," in his words.

To this day, I don't know where the hands went as we wrestled on the bed. I can't tell you for sure whether or not either competitor was aroused. The heat would be turned up, the sweat would pour off us, and soon the shirts would come off.

It wasn't until I had kids of my own that I reframed what had become a very dark picture of the relationship I had with Brother Dwight. Though I didn't realize it at the time, the writing of *Collared* was not only my way of processing the sordid details of sex abuse in my beloved church that spewed off the pages of *The Boston Globe*; it was also my way of making sense of how a predator had preyed on my family. Writing that last sentence just now put the charge of anger in me yet again, which probably explains why the body count of clergy in my little story is so shockingly high.

My parents sat there silent for a long moment. The thrill of holding my newborn book was now replaced by soul-sucking dread: It was bad enough that these hardworking churchgoers had been hoodwinked by a man of the cloth whom they revered; now they were going to go through the humiliation of having a son go on a book tour and broadcast this to the world?

"I'm having dinner with Dwight tonight, and that's when he's going to get his copy," I said.

My mother's mood brightened.

"Oh, good!" she exclaimed. "You know, he had broken his ankle and I never sent anything over to him, not even a fruit basket. You think you could stop somewhere in your travels and get him something? I'll pay yeh back."

My father, a Tuam man not one to make a lot of noise, erupted.

"Did yeh not hear a thing he just said? Jesus!"

I'm not sure what she heard, and to this day, she has chosen not to read the book. She did, however, attend every book signing as a show of support, because that is the choice cut of a woman she is. Questioning one's faith and its clergy was not a match for her rural Irish upbringing, and I've decided to let her respond to this in her own way. When she's ready to talk about it, I am here to listen.

I drove over to the pub across the street from my old high school and grabbed the copy of *Collared* in the passenger's seat, tucking it into my satchel before I walked inside.

He entered the bar area, and the ruddy cheeks on his smooth face brightened at the sight of me as he waved. I got up and we hugged briefly before he removed his coat and straightened the collar on his cassock. My eyes lingered on the large cross on his neck, and I wondered if I was doing His work with this book nonsense.

"You decided to wear the full-on black dress, I see?"

"I'll do anything for a free drink," he replied with a laugh. "We're going to need a lot of drinks tonight, baby! There's a lot to celebrate."

"Oh?"

"I just signed a book deal with a publisher on my doctoral thesis," he gushed; scarcely able to get the words out fast enough. "It's going to be made into a textbook!"

I pulled *Collared* from my bag and slid it across the table.

"Looks like we both have books to celebrate," I said.

His eyes focused on the cover as his well-manicured hands rested on the binding.

"Pretty dark—what—is that a hand over the throat?" he observed. "Wow. What's it about?"

"There's a nice summary if you flip it over."

The pinkness of his cheeks faded as he took in each sentence. I caught a flash of panic in his eyes before he bowed his head and thumbed through the pages.

"Is this about me?" he stammered.

"It's not about you, but yet you're all over the book all the same," I said evenly. "Now that I'm a parent myself, I am starting to reflect on the horsing around you did with me as a kid on those vacations, in those hotel rooms, and I began thinking to myself, *If someone ever did that to my kid, I'd probably blow their fucking head off.*"

"But I..."

I held my palm a few inches from his face and he recoiled.

"Stop. Don't comment on something you haven't read yet," I said. Now it was my turn to stammer. "Why don't we meet up when you're done with this and we can continue the discussion then, okay?"

I threw a twenty-dollar bill on the table.

"That should cover my drinks and a few of your own as you celebrate both books." My heart thumped in my chest and drummed in my ear like a spin cycle with an unbalanced load of towels.

A few weeks later, there was a message on my answering machine from Dwight. He was visiting some nun friends of his in the parish one town over and was wondering if we could meet for a drink.

This time, he was there first to greet me. The hug we exchanged was stiff and clumsy, like two clashing marionettes whose strings were hopelessly tangled. I sat down and ordered a drink from the bartender. Dwight did the same before sliding the book over to me.

"You forgot to sign it," he said with a wide grin.

"What did you think of it?"

"I'm proud of you, man. It was well-written. I really couldn't put it down."

"That's all?"

He cleared his throat.

"I could see what you meant about me being all over the book. I felt the anger. I just want to apologize, Mike. Really. You were like the little brother I never had. I was just playing around with you like brothers do. I never intended it to be anything more than that, but now that I read it, I can see that this caused you hurt. I really feel awful about that."

"My parents didn't deserve what you dished out," I said, my throat tightening as it usually does during confrontation.

"What did I dish out?" he asked defensively. "I told you: I was just playing around back then. Is what I did inappropriate by today's standards, when every Tom, Dick, and Harry is suing everyone else? Absolutely! Are there things that I did back then that this fifty-year-old would never do today? Absolutely! But really, all that was going on, at least from my end, was just some innocent fun, and I'm sorry if it landed in some other way for you. You have to believe me that there was nothing weird or sexual going on."

Before I could continue, the nuns joined us at the bar. Brother

Dwight proudly displayed the book that his "cousin" wrote. The beer and cocktails came fast and furious, the vow of poverty no match for the direct billing the bar did for the parish. "You've got balls for writing this, I'll give you that," said one portly nun who swayed ominously and slurred each word.

"Those fucking 'princes of the parish' deserve everything that's coming their way. They ruined everything for the rest of us."

The next morning, I poured another cup of coffee in a useless attempt to shake off the previous night's hangover, and somewhere in the haze I concluded that I was satisfied with both his explanation and the apology I had received, which paved the way for me to place the experience in the rearview mirror.

But my book had other plans for me.

A few newspapers reprinted the press release from my publisher, and I got a few publicity nibbles once it was released, and word slowly got out within my high school alumni community about *Collared*. A few familiar faces stood in line to buy the book at my readings. It opened old wounds in others just as I was healing my own, and other graduates came forward to lodge formal complaints to the religious order about Dwight. The order ejected Dwight from his position as director of religious education in that parish school in the shadows of JFK Airport, and placed him in the brothers' retirement house, away from children, until the investigation was over. They hired a private investigative firm to help them separate the facts from the bogus claims, and the publicity from the book led the order to have the firm contact me. We exchanged emails and picked a time and a place to meet.

I took one look at the ruler-straight posture, starched shirt, and perfectly perpendicular tie bar on the guy in the corner of the Starbucks on this casual Sunday morning and I knew I had my man. The private investigator shook my hand firmly, thanked me for my time, and acknowledged how difficult this line of questioning would likely be for me. He opened his leather-clad notebook and wrote my name and the date on the next blank page in precise block letters.

If processing one's feelings through a fictional device were a fine chardonnay diluted in a swimming pool, this interrogation was a fifth of *poitín*. Each question drew back the memory curtains. The investigator was most interested in my relationship with this man of the cloth so woven into the fabric of my childhood that he made it into my last extended-family portrait.

"When did the abuse happen and for how long?"

"It started when I was about fifteen, and I'd say it lasted about a year or two."

The questions kept coming.

"How many times and in what locations did you find yourself alone in a hotel room with him?"

"How much alcohol was involved?"

"So, he asked you to take off your shirt before you started wrestling on the bed again—then what happened?"

He leaned in and said, "Say more about that" from time to time, and I did. Each answer I gave shined fog lights through these murky roads of the past.

I was once again confronted by the depth of my family's betrayal at the hands of this alleged "man of God," and my stomach tightened. I excused myself, did a few dry heaves into the toilet, and returned to my chair.

A question like "Were you ever in the car with him alone?" brought back a memory I hadn't had in thirty years. I remembered the excitement of first getting my driver's license and being all too happy to drive over to my high school to take Brother Dwight out for pizza. My father would throw money at me for gas, dinner, and "a little extra money for himself, since the poor fella took the vow of poverty and all." We would have our pizza and I would split the extra money Dad gave with him; Dwight wasn't the only one operating under the veil of poverty in those days. It made me think of the amount of overtime Dad had to work for the twenties he peeled from his wallet, and a wave of rage tumbled in me again.

How could I have been so stupid?

I was numb on my way home and barely had time to park the car in the driveway before the phone rang again. The private investigator realized I had a difficult day and sheepishly asked if there were any pictures placing me with Dwight in these hotels.

I flipped through yellowed pages of one of the photo albums stacked in the basement. Lies. Lies! *Lies!!* The broad grin on his face is now a crocodile's smile when I cast this thirty-year-old picture in a new frame. The weight of this sticky, layered muck of deceit bent me until I found myself on the floor, sobbing uncontrollably.

Brother Dwight had the nerve to contact my parents. He left a message on their answering machine, asking them to call him back so that he could apologize. My parents were distraught, and I was consumed with rage. Though I despise the litigiousness of our society, I called the private investigator with a message for the order: If we got one more phone call from Dwight, I would not rest until I owned every blade of grass on school property. That was the last contact the family has had with him.

I thought writing *Collared* put everything behind me and that I was whole and complete with everything that had happened, but the tangle with the private investigator revealed that there was more work to do. Where to start?

My first breakthrough occurred when I asked my daughter over dinner one night if there would be any cute boys at the high school dance she was attending that evening. Her back stiffened. She seemed unsure about what to do with the torrent of strange hormones and the new feelings about the opposite sex that came with it. I saw myself in her face at that moment, and it dawned on me that she was about my age when all this happened, before the Internet and three decades before any of the church scandals came to light. The unformed sexuality. The questions that had no answers at the time. The lack of experience. I was hardly in a position to know what was going on myself, let alone protect anyone else around me. I was sick and tired of the guilt and shame; wasn't it time to forgive myself for just being a naive teen who didn't have the luxury of search engines to seek the answers I needed?

The more difficult step involved forgiving Brother Dwight. I was always inspired by the strength Pope John Paul II showed when he made the pilgrimage to forgive Mehmet Ali Agca, the jailed man who had made an attempt on his life. But John Paul II was aiming to be a saint—and I ain't. Could I ever be that strong?

In flipping through the research I'd amassed for *Collared* all those years ago, I read again the research papers that pointed to a pattern of sex abuse in a pedophile's own past. Other research speculated about whether a traumatic brain injury could cause this deviant behavior.

Maybe he visited the physical or emotional pain from his own childhood upon other children. I recalled the bigoted, outsized personality of his father and easily sketched out a new villain in this scenario. I didn't know his background well enough to be sure that any of this was true, and even if it was, it certainly didn't excuse his behavior. But the story proved useful as I attempted to find a new wellspring of forgiveness, and in doing so, I was able to let go of any lingering anger and regret. I thought my work was finally done.

Once again, *Collared* had other plans.

I eagerly accepted the invitation to my thirtieth high school reunion, in part to gratify my ego. I had a beautiful wife, a powerful life, a reduced waistline, and a burgeoning literary career to present to the old bullies and teachers who never thought I'd amount to anything. A former thug who tormented me on the school bus brought a book for me to sign and gushed like a teenager in my presence, confirming the wisdom in my decision.

There was another man with a copy of *Collared* in the room; he was one of the religious brothers. The years had piled blubber onto his frame and his body was fighting cancer, but his blue eyes hadn't lost an ounce of their intensity.

"I brought Dwight into this order as vocation director, and I blame myself for everything that happened to you and your family," he said as he produced the novel for me to sign. "I can't tell you how sorry I am for the pain I caused."

It was evident that a cone of silence enveloped these men of the cloth, who were no doubt spooked by my recent and regrettable threat of legal action. The mild-mannered physics teacher leaked some details about Dwight in a weak moment. The investigation revealed a pattern of behavior reproduced in the testimonies of four other former students. Dwight got sloppy in his older years, leaving a trail of text messages that a recent graduate of the school shared with the order. An offer for counseling was made to Dwight and rejected, and the order separated from him. A rumor went around the religious order that a family friend of Dwight's kept a large inheritance from his parents in a marked account, which was inconsistent with the vow of poverty but certainly came in handy at a time like this. A one-sentence email announced this to the order, and no one has heard from him since.

"Our students are like our children," said another one of the brothers, who pulled me into a corner of the room to bare his soul while my classmates all around us reminisced about the good old days. "Dwight duped us all, and it's hard to live with the fact that this happened on our watch."

"That's nice of you not to sue us, but if you do, I'll be the first one in the fucking witness box with my right hand raised," bellowed yet another brother as we took a tour around campus. "Maybe you can sue the order to take his goddamned picture off the walls of the brothers' residence—I get nauseous looking at it."

In each case, I found myself reassuring them that I harbored no ill will against the order, and then acknowledging the immeasurable contribution these men of faith made to the man I am today.

Being in a position to provide comfort to these heartbroken, angry men was real power, and the label of "abuse victim" no longer applied from that moment. Letting go of being Irish freed me from the shackles of resentment and regret and allowed me to be a source of freedom for others.

If that's not the delicious fruit of a successful writing career, I don't know what is!

Give my regards to Broadway,
Remember me to Herald Square,
Tell all the gang at 42nd Street,
That I will soon be there;

Whisper of how I'm yearning
To mingle with the old time throng,
Give my regards to old Broadway,
And say that I'll be there e'er long.

## George M. Cohan

*(July 3, 1878—November 5, 1942)*

# Malachy McCourt

Malachy McCourt was born in Brooklyn in 1931. He was raised in Limerick with his seven siblings, the younger brother of Frank McCourt. He returned to New York in his teens and took a job as a longshoreman. McCourt owned a legendary saloon on the East Side of Manhattan. He ran for governor of New York in 2006, losing to Eliot Spitzer. He is also an actor, appearing in numerous feature movies and television shows. He has written several memoirs, among them the *New York Times* best seller *A Monk Swimming*. His latest book, *Death Need Not Be Fatal*, was published in 2017. McCourt lives in Manhattan with his wife of more than fifty years, Diana.

# A New York Writer!

Being a writer in New York is quite similar to being a writer in the Sahara Desert, except of course for the possession of the writing implements. Not being computer competent, I am strictly a pen-and-paper man prior to anything getting in publishable print. Getting down to the actual writing, which means sitting down, picking up the pen, placing the writing end of the same at the top of the threatening blank page of paper, and pondering the birth of a word that sets me off on this creative journey, seems an impossible task, not at all easy. If you are in the Sahara, there are a number of tasks essential to life that have to be completed before you set down the words. There is a tent rope that has frayed and has to be replaced, and the water from the local oasis looks a bit slimy and has to be boiled. One of the camels has diarrhea and has left you a smelly gift at the entrance to your tent, which has to be removed. Sand has gotten into your teacup and has to be rinsed. Your fountain pen is out of ink and the point of your pencil is not sharp enough. You suddenly remember that you were supposed to start a revolution in Saudi Arabia about women driving and that was yesterday and now it's too late. You *vow* that you will sit down tomorrow for sure to write. At dawn, goddammit.

If you are in New York City and in the writing business, it's hopeless. The streets are clogged with novelists, essayists, journalists, commentators, screenwriters, playwrights, humorists, economists, editorialists, all on their way to publishers to magazines to agents, clutching the fruits of their labors, that manuscript of the most magnificent original piece of writing to crash into the glittering literary world since the first issue of *Hustler*, so what hope is there for me to get published?

As for myself, I am merely an author who has a very famous

brother who was a writer. Fortunately my stuff is easy to read, and though as I said I'm swinging in on my brother's coattails, various editors like my writing.

## 2

Professional writers have a disciplined routine. One writer whose name is not in my noggin arose in the morning, had breakfast with the spouse, went and got dressed in a business suit, polished shoes, school tie, picked up his briefcase, kissed his wife, and left for his office, which was in his basement down one flight of stairs, where he stayed for the day. I on the other hand am a perennial procrastinator. The two prime areas of procrastination for me are dying and writing. Putting off the dying is number-one priority for me, as I want to get my last book written, *I Read Your Brother's Book,* and get a goodly advance for same.

Regarding death, the only reason organized religion infects so many people is fear of death and hell. With that in mind, I discussed with one publisher the possibility of securing a large advance on the book I would like to write posthumously. He looked at me quizzically, one might even say warily, as if I had taken leave of my senses, and he said, "But that has never been done." I thundered back with the great cliché "There is always a first time." The publisher found he had argent businesses to attend to and he hastily departed.

There are many more of these divergences before I can sit down and write. As I use a fountain pen, there are certain formalities to be observed. The pen has to be unearthed from the place I am certain I would never leave a valuable fountain pen. Then the ink bottle has to be found and you'll know someone in the house has moved it. The intensive search ends when I find the ink bottle in the very place where I had left it behind the dictionary on the desk. The task of refilling the pen leaves my fingers splattered with ink, my trousers all spattered with same, and various books and papers in the vicinity are evidence that I have filled my fountain pen close by.

Then there is no way of completing anything without a cup of green tea and a fraction of a cracker and cheddar cheese.

Of course there is that phone call from Bob asking how I am which has to be returned. And my membership in Symphony Space will expire in about six months and has to be renewed and right now. It's November and I'm wondering what dates next September Adrianna goes back to college and there are some soiled dishes in the sink (I never say dirty dishes because we don't eat dirt on dishes), plus I have to look up the showtimes of that movie next Sunday.

I am like one of those baseball pitchers who peers intently at the catcher, scratches his head many times, and finally nods then pulls his cap down then pushes it up then pulls it down again then pushes it up, moves it to the side, moves it back to the original side, then chews on something and spits, chews again and spits again, wipes his mouth with his sleeve, throws the ball to first base, and when he retrieves it, makes every effort with both hands to make it rounder than the manufacturer intended. After rounding the ball by vigorously pressing it between his palms, the pitcher will attend to that other ball game. His right hand will descend to his testicles and with a series of rapid movements he will attempt to reinvigorate two other balls that are hanging dormant between his legs. And his hand will return to the job of restructuring the baseball by the usual twisting and pressing. He will then fling the ball, and even if he does not hit anything, it will despite the evidence be called a strike. It's all very public evidence of procrastination, which is a comfort to every writer. Of course watching baseball is mere procrastination itself.

Writers in the Sahara do not have any critics to contend with, as camels generally speaking cannot read, just like the average conservative. Whereas in New York, critics abound, conservatives, like camels, are illiterate, but they still express their opinions even though people stopped reading to them a long time ago.

Yet eventually I get to sit down, unlike Hemingway who stood to write, pick up the eager pen, and somehow or another words are written on the blank page. I am in no position to judge whether my words are worthy, because that's not my place. I frequently say, Never judge your work, for you will always find it guilty, and never show anything to blood relatives, for they would find you guilty of every lie ever told.

Having been in the acting trade, and used to an immediate reaction from audiences, sitting alone in solitary silence, there is no curtain call, there is no applause, no laughter, no groans, pats on the back, not even criticism, there is just a page in front of you which seems to be saying, *So what!* Even if you are lucky as I was to have my friend Charlie DiFanti get me published, you run into critics of all stripes all the time. Some will say, "Your book was disgusting, I threw it in the waste with the coffee grounds. You are no Frank McCourt!" George Bernard Shaw said critics are like eunuchs in a harem. They see it done, they know how it's done, but they can't do it. Most writers do get eunuch-itis once in a while, but all you have to do is keep writing. At times I write blather just to fill the page with obscenities, including all of George Carlin's dirty words that can't be said on television, and then the blood gets flowing like ink and off we go on our rollicking journey and what does it matter after the words have departed your pen? I tried to dodge the issue of procrastination by saying I am not really a writer, an obvious prevarication of the truth, as you are reading my writing.

I say, go now and write your book, there is always hope.

# Frank O'Hara

*(March 27, 1926—July 25, 1966)*

Who knows what madness transpires to create an artist! In the case of Frank O'Hara, it could be argued that the seeds of his discontent were sown at the very outset of his life. He was born in a quiet suburb of Baltimore on the 26th of March, 1926, to Russell and Katherine O'Hara. His parents both came from strict Irish Catholic families, and for years they lied to Frank, telling him that his birthdate was June 27, 1926, to hide the fact that he was conceived out of wedlock.

At the age of eighteen, he went off for two years to serve in the U.S. Navy, where he was a sonar man on the destroyer USS *Nicholas* during World War II. After just two years in the service, O'Hara was able to attend Harvard on the GI Bill, where he roomed with artist Edward Gorey and met poet John Ashberry. He and Ashberry hit it off, and in 1951, while still at Harvard, O'Hara published his first collection of poems, *A Byzantine Place*, which won a major Hopwood Award at the University of Michigan.

Later that same year, he and Ashberry moved to New York City and rented an apartment together. O'Hara got a job as an assistant to photographer Cecil Beaton before finding a full-time job at the Museum of Modern Art, where he manned the front desk, selling tickets and postcards while scribbling poems in his notebook every chance he could.

O'Hara made many important friends in the art world during his time at the museum: Jackson Pollock, Willem de Kooning, and Kenneth Koch. Together with Ashberry and a handful of others, they became part of an informal group of artists known as the New York School.

It was on the streets of New York that O'Hara found his voice. Whereas previous generations of poets had found sustenance and inspiration in nature, O'Hara found his muse in the hustle and bustle of the metropolis. He turned the haphazard chaos of everyday voices and street imagery into linguistic snapshots of the city he loved. His poetry reads like an urban form of word jazz, a poetic abstract expressionism. He scribbled poems on napkins and scraps of paper and shoved them carelessly in his pockets or in drawers to be forgotten. He was interested only in the moment; snap, discard, repeat, like a human camera.

He loved New York. The hectic, haphazard buzz of the city suited his fiery synapses. The chaos of the street inspired his imagination, and the openness of the artistic community fueled his passion. He was one of the first poets of his generation to live openly as a gay man, inspiring countless others to follow his lead.

But O'Hara's reckless pursuit of love, life, and alcohol caught up with him early. He was hit by a joy-riding dune buggy on a Fire Island beach at 2:40 on the morning of July 24, 1966, after a day drinking with friends. He was only forty years old. At his funeral, the artist Larry Rivers elicited gasps of horror from the congregation with his graphic account of O'Hara's mangled body in the hospital in the days following the accident. But perhaps O'Hara would have appreciated his old friend's attention to detail, the attempt at capturing the broken fragments of what remained of his life, the purple skin, the white hospital gown, the dark blue thread…snap.

Frank O'Hara posthumously won the National Book Award for poetry in 1972.

Colin Broderick

# Don Creedon

Don Creedon, originally from Dublin, has appeared on stage in Irish productions all over New York. He is the co-founder and Artistic Director of The Poor Mouth Theatre Company in Riverdale, New York. He has written numerous plays, among them *The Lobby*, *Celtic Tiger me Arse,* and *Guy Walks into a Bar*, which received the Audience Award for Best Play at the 1st Irish 2010 Theatre Festival in Manhattan.

# Reading and Writing

In November 1985, I landed the perfect job for an aspiring actor: New York City doorman. Although I'd left Dublin for New York only two months before, I was quickly running out of acceptable ways of making a living. I'd already gone through three different jobs. Bartending was just way too much work, waiting tables even worse, and as for construction, forget it. But a young illegal alien doesn't have much choice. My enthusiasm for this new adventure was fading fast, until I arrived at the American Felt Building.

"That's it?" I asked. "That's all I have to do?"

The Irish super nodded.

"Cool," I said as I perused the stark interior of the converted loft building. Very chic, very minimalist, very eighties. Very fucking perfect.

Basically, the job entailed sitting down for eight hours a night, five nights a week. There was a catch; I had to wear a doorman's uniform. But they weren't fooling me—I knew it wasn't a uniform; it was a costume. I was only going to be pretending to be a doorman. What I really was going to be doing was…reading. Yes, long epic novels, the longer and more tragic the better, especially by the Russians. *War and Peace, Crime and Punishment, The Idiot, Anna Karenina.* I was going to be spending my nights with some of the most tragic, depressing stories ever written. I was in heaven. The other perfect thing about the job was that it freed up my days for auditions.

At that time, the only professional Irish theater in Manhattan was the Irish Arts Center, so that's where I headed. After helping out backstage with a few productions, I landed my first professional acting role almost a year later in a production of *The Tunnel,* a new play about an escape attempt from Long

Kesh H-Block prison, set during the height of the Troubles in Northern Ireland. The play was written by Gregory Teer, whose real name, I soon discovered, was Terry George. (Because of Terry's background in Northern Ireland, he insisted on this pseudonym, an anagram of his real name.) The cast included Frank McCourt. It was directed by Jim Sheridan.

Most of October was spent in rehearsals. The script was powerful, very direct and hard-hitting. The world depicted within the walls of Long Kesh felt authentic and real, and the action built to a satisfying climax. But Jim and Terry seemed less convinced. There was a lot of head-scratching and confabs between director and writer. I shrugged, simply happy to be working with such a talented group. We opened in early November to a lukewarm reception and closed before Thanksgiving. And that, I thought, was that; back to Tolstoy and Dostoyevsky.

Until I got word over Christmas that we were "goin' at it again." So in I came for more rehearsals in January, for what I thought would just be a quick tune-up, only to be greeted by a totally revised script. Some of my favorite speeches had been thrown out, backstories added, characters combined, while others eliminated entirely (thankfully not mine!). Once again, we delved into rehearsals and opened for a second time, two weeks later. This time the reviews were raves. According to *The New York Times*, Jim Sheridan "had achieved the utmost verisimilitude." Jim joked, "Does this mean he thought it was any good?" We played to full houses and ran for another six months.

This experience was a revelation to me. Up to then, I'd naively assumed that a play was something created by a playwright working alone, usually in a single, creative burst. I had some vague notion of "the Artist" toiling for months in his garret, then emerging, clutching his finished manuscript like some half-demented character in…well, a Russian novel. As to whatever happened in this garret, it was something mysterious, inspired by the Muse, granted only to the chosen few. Yet here, before my eyes, Terry and Jim had somehow taken this play apart and put it back together again better than ever. How had they done this? If this wasn't the moment I became a writer, it was certainly the moment I first realized that maybe someday I could.

So began a very hectic period of my life; hanging out with the Russians every night until seven in the morning, sleeping until three in the afternoon, rehearsals or performances in the evening, then dashing back for my nightly rendezvous with the Russians at eleven. During these years, I acted in so many productions it was hard to keep track, everything from roles in revivals of Irish plays like *The Plough and the Stars* to playing a Farmer in *Oklahoma!* But the two standout experiences along the way were *Away Alone*, by Janet Noble, and *Down the Flats*, by Tony Kavanagh. And again, just like *The Tunnel*, these were new works being performed for the first time. Although neither play demanded the kind overhaul undertaken with *The Tunnel*, the rehearsal process was the same, an open engagement back and forth between writer and director, trying to realize on stage what had previously existed only on the page. I found this collaboration fascinating and listened to every word. More and more, it seemed I was becoming interested in the bigger picture, seeing the play from the perspective of the writer and the director.

During this same period, I'd also gotten married, and when my daughter was born a couple of years later, we moved from the city to Dobbs Ferry in Westchester County. By this time, I'd given up the pretense of being a doorman and was now pretending to be a desktop publisher in midtown Manhattan. Family life and the demands of a full-time day job were making it harder and harder to find time for auditions and rehearsals, let alone perform six or seven shows a week. But my daily commute on Metro-North from Dobbs Ferry did provide me with a new opportunity: thirty-four minutes each way, exactly one hour and eight minutes of uninterrupted, dedicated time every day in which to write.

So I wrote every day on the train. I'd had an idea for a play, you see, which was to be set in the lobby of a converted loft building, and the main character was to be a young aspiring writer from Dublin in the guise of a certain Irish doorman.

By chance, my move to Dobbs Ferry coincided with the creation of the Irish Bronx Theatre Company (IBTC) in the early nineties, founded by two wonderfully gifted actors, Jimmy Smallhorne and Chris O'Neill, both of whom I'd worked with in *Down the Flats*. Jimmy's and Chris's energy and passion for theater was infectious, and their timing was perfect. The huge wave of Irish emigration to the U.S. during the eighties had resulted in a burgeoning young Irish population in New York, many of them drawn to the Irish enclaves in Woodlawn, Yonkers, and parts of Bainbridge and Riverdale. This young crowd regularly flocked to the IBTC on Bainbridge Avenue to see revivals of popular Irish plays like *Da, The Country Boy, The Risen People*, and *Away Alone*. At the same time, over in Riverdale, Dubliner Dermot Burke opened An Beal Bocht Café in 1991, and in a few short months "the Beal" had established itself as the preeminent venue for new music, poetry, and play readings. The Bronx was no longer simply an affordable place for the Irish who wanted to live in the city. By the mid-nineties it had become a destination in its own right.

Although the IBTC folded somewhat prematurely, with the untimely death of Chris O'Neill, the seeds had already been sown. A group of actors, myself included, went on to form Macalla Theatre Company in 1994, with the mission to bring new Irish plays, never before seen in the U.S., to this audience in Woodlawn, the Bronx. Our first production was the U.S. premiere of *Tuesday's Child,* a little gem of a play about a pregnant young teenager who's convinced beyond a shadow of a doubt that her unborn child has been immaculately conceived. The play also features a live chicken. This was to be my first attempt at directing, and thankfully I was gifted with the perfect cast, who, despite my efforts, managed to deliver wonderful performances, even in the case of the chicken.

By this time, the daily Metro-North writing plan had yielded a complete first draft of my play, *The Lobby,* a comedy farce about a group of young Irish twenty-somethings jostling for their place in the big city. When Macalla went looking for a second play, someone asked if I happened to know of any new play that had a lot of parts for young actors, preferably Irish, maybe even set in New York? "Well, now, since you ask…"

"Jaysis, Don, this fuckin' play of yours better be good, 'cos we won't get away with any avant-gardey shite in this neighborhood."

This was Paddy Sheanon. Paddy was playing Tock, the very troublesome and unruly house painter in *The Lobby.* He was well cast. Just like Tock, Paddy was incapable of editing himself—every thought that entered his head came tumbling out in a stream of unsolicited reports, like a commentator who forgot to turn his mike off. It was moments before opening night of my very first play—probably the most frightening few moments of my life—and Paddy and I were eyeing the audience from safely behind the curtain. The "theater" was the basement of a church on 240th Street and Martha Avenue in Woodlawn. As director, I'd spent the best part of the previous month with Paddy and the rest of the cast rehearsing in the basement of the Heritage, a nearby pub on McLean Avenue. The house was full; Barry's tea, Tayto crisps, and Cadbury's Crunchies were selling fast as people craned their necks from their folding chairs. As the houselights dimmed, Paddy tried to be positive.

"Don't worry, Don. You'll soon know if they don't like it. We don't do polite applause in the Bronx."If I thought I was nervous, Johnnie McConnell, one of the other actors, was even worse. It was his first time ever on stage, and Johnnie was a bag of nerves. That night, he took his final exit with a look of horror on his face.

"That's it," he croaked. "I'm never going back out there again!"

But I was barely listening. The only thing I could hear was applause; the loudest, most impolite applause I'd ever heard.

"You bloody better go back out, Johnnie. You haven't taken your curtain call."

*The Lobby* ran to full houses in the Bronx for another three weeks. It seemed like Johnnie had about three heart attacks every night, and every time he came off, he swore he'd never go back on. At the end of the run, he vowed never to darken the door of a theater again.

"Only one problem, Johnnie," I said. "We open again next week, at the Irish Arts Center."

So open again we did, for another three weeks in Manhattan. And yes, Johnnie went on again too, for one last time; the same Johnnie who was to appear on Broadway in *The Weir* just four years later.

The success of *The Lobby* was followed by other Macalla productions through the mid-nineties, many directed by me. By 1998, the economic tide had turned in Ireland's favor with the economic phenomenon known as the Celtic Tiger, enticing many emigrants to return home to take advantage of the new opportunities. My second play, *Celtic Tiger, Me Arse,* satirized this trend, depicting a newly married couple eagerly returning to Ireland only to be greeted by a brash new society obsessed with real estate values. This play had a successful run at the

Irish Arts Center during 1999 and also at the Celtic Arts Center in L.A. in 2001.

Unlike many people I knew, I was never tempted to return. The truth is I'd loved New York from the moment I landed at JFK. The energy and enthusiasm of the place lifted me right away, and honestly, I think I needed the encouragement. Despite Ireland's reputation as a home for the arts, the Ireland I grew up in, in the sixties and seventies, had always told me to "be sensible," to "settle down" and not have too many "notions about myself." New York, on the other hand, told me to be myself, even if I didn't know exactly who that was. "Don't worry," it said. "You'll discover it along the way."

So I stayed, and, as many predicted, the Celtic Tiger eventually roared itself hoarse and whimpered off into the sunset. Not long afterwards, Dermot Burke and his business partner Tony Caffrey expanded An Beal Bocht Café in Riverdale into the storefront next door, and when their good friend the writer Colin Broderick saw the new space, he immediately recognized it as the perfect home for a new theater company. He quickly called Stephen Smallhorne and me. We didn't need to be asked twice.

This was the birth of the Poor Mouth Theatre Company, which Colin, Stephen, and I founded together in March 2010. To this day, Poor Mouth continues to actively support new playwriting by Irish writers based here in New York, with an ongoing commitment to the development process, producing short plays, workshops, readings, works-in-progress, and, of course, fully fledged pieces. It has served as the launching pad for new works by playwrights such as Seamus Scanlan, Brona Crehan, and Stephen Smallhorne, plays that have gone on to productions in Manhattan and beyond, including my own *Guy Walks Into a Bar,* which won the Audience Award for Best Play at Origin Theater's first Irish Theater Festival in 2010. When it comes to theater (or indeed, all artistic endeavor), I believe it's really about what I discovered back on that January day with *The Tunnel:* The process is essential. And that process, I think, is reiterative; an ongoing, open engagement with the work, the fundamental aspect of which is a kind of listening. Even the act of writing itself is not really writing but rewriting. My own practice is that I write and then rewrite until it no longer makes me wince. So I don't really have to be a good writer, I only have to be a good reader. And whether Tolstoy or Dostoyevsky or my own humble efforts, reading is something I've always loved to do.

"Once there was another city here, and now it is gone. There are almost no traces of it anymore, but millions of us know it existed, because we lived in it: the Lost City of New York."

—*New York* magazine

# *Pete Hamill*
*(Born June 24, 1935)*

# Maura Mulligan

Maura Mulligan emigrated to America from County Mayo in 1958. She was a telephone operator for the New York Telephone Company until she answered a higher call to become a nun in 1962. After leaving religious life, she taught in New York City schools after earning an M.A. at Hunter College of the City University of New York. Mulligan was awarded a writer's residency at Achill Island's Heinrich Böll Cottage in 2009. Her memoir, *Call of the Lark*, was published in 2012. She currently teaches céilí dance and is at work on playwriting.

# A Late Bloomer

My writer's voice awoke on wild and beautiful Achill Island, which juts out into the North Atlantic from the coast of County Mayo. It was 1995, and I was in my fifties.

You might think that someone born in a thatched cottage in rural County Mayo would have had an earlier start. It's possible I could have found my voice in 1962, if the path I'd chosen then nurtured creativity instead of self-denial and custody of the senses.

As a young nun at Ladycliff College in Highland Falls, New York, I wrote a composition about a skylark. The instructor praised my work, advising me to develop my voice. But nurturing creativity and personal awareness was not high on the convent to-do list in those days before Vatican II. In fact, creativity and appreciation of self-worth were under attack for those of us who answered "the call."

Focus was on rituals like the Chapter of Faults, a not-to-be-missed novitiate practice that had us on our knees accusing ourselves of transgressions such as breaking silence, dropping a dish, or (in my own case) dancing in the hallway to uplift my spirits.

Penance rituals to bring about humility and crush individuality especially during Lent included a Good Friday custom that had an ironic outcome for some of us who were young. Picking at my food while kneeling on the floor and trying to keep my plate away from the shoes of the sister in front of me was a humorous challenge. *If only everyone would hurry up and finish their fish so I could get up and defrost my knees* was what I thought about.

These practices, presumed to diminish pride and worldliness, didn't even banish vanity. In the absence of mirrors, those of us who wanted to remember what we still looked like tried to find our reflections in the shiny acrylic light switch plate at the entrance to the chapel. We were shallow, Mother Mistress, the head nun, told us.

These memories rose up and presented themselves to be written down, but not for a long time after I left the religious order, and not until I had first written about my childhood in Ireland.

Visiting my native Aghamore in east Mayo on a gray day in 1995, I wandered around the ruins of what was once my family home. Thistles and weeds covered the stony yard where chickens had fluttered their wings and gathered round my mother's laced-up boots whenever she emerged from the red half door with a bucket of feed in her hands. I could hear the wind close the door with a bang just as it did when we ran in and out to play hide-and-seek among the haycocks in the front field. The gap where that door once hung was now filled with briars and long weeds. The flagged floor where I had practiced my dance steps to the Gallow Glass Céilí Band playing on the gramophone was covered with grass.

In this space, which now had the darkening sky for a roof, I wondered how in the world a table, four chairs, and a cradle had fit along with my parents, two sisters, and three brothers as they came along in turn. My father, like most small farmers at that time, did seasonal labor in England. When he came home for a visit, he left my mother with a bigger belly. Nine months later, "a baby was found under a head of cabbage."

My siblings and I had all emigrated to New York and London, so these ruins of my childhood home now belonged to someone else, who was getting rid of the stones, preparing what was now his land for tillage. Here, I felt the presence of my sister Mag, who, at age thirty-seven, had suffered a stroke and died in New York. I thought of my two younger brothers, P.J. and Tommie, who had passed away within a few years of each other. They had lived in London, where alcohol became their best friend and then took them away.

The bulldozer parked near the ash tree I had climbed as a small girl would soon, I knew, reach out to devour my childhood memories buried in those remaining stones.

I had given up on the religious life, but not on prayer. The Ecclesiastes reminded me that there is a time for everything. Dance had always made me hopeful and strong, so I headed for Scoil Acla (the Achill summer school). The dance class was to start the following week, so I joined a writing class while waiting to dance.

Under the encouraging tutelage of the late poet Macdara Woods, who told me to close my eyes and listen to the silence, I wrote lines about childhood memories and about dancing on flagged stones. It was a time to write.

Wanting to discover more about this newfound art, I determined to join a class when I returned to New York. There I met writer Ellen Schecter, author of the inspiring memoir *Fierce Joy*, and joined her, Dan Rouss, Diana Kash, and others in a supportive group that I found to be a nurturing experience for my developing skills.

For a few years, I focused on childhood in Ireland and my first years in America, when I worked as a long-distance operator for the New York Telephone Company. I was hesitant to share anything about the day I answered a higher call. This non-Catholic writing group without a drop of Irish blood in their collective veins would not understand, I reasoned. But these writers helped me realize that the convent stories blended with my childhood life. My immigrant experience, they reminded me, had a universal appeal.

Hilda, RIP, tried to encourage me further by comparing the Jewish practice of a married woman covering her hair with a wig to the nun replacing her hair with a veil. I disagreed about it being a good comparison on the grounds that the Jewish woman kept her own hair under the wig and slept with her husband. The nun, especially if a member of an order founded in Italy, as was the community I'd been a member of, was expected to rid herself of "impure thoughts." This, we were told, could be accomplished by using "the discipline," a chainlike device for beating oneself. My chain stayed in its little black silk purse and never saw the light of day. I thought, as did others of my time, that the custom was beyond archaic.

The group was particularly wowed with the ritual of becoming a bride of Christ—when I wore a white wedding dress and veil, walked down the aisle, and prostrated myself along with twenty-six other young women in front of the altar. It was when we were covered with a black shroud and the knell of the bell announced our death to the world that some parents at the ceremony cried, mourning their loss. Others rejoiced because of the great honor of having a daughter called to the religious life. My own mother couldn't afford to come for the ceremony, but if she'd been there, I imagine she'd have turned to the mourners and told them to whisht. She'd have spoken up and reminded them that we new nuns "will not have a care in the world, being married to the Lord."

"You must include all this in your book," said group member David Perez, who was writing about his time as a Catholic-school student in the Bronx. David has since published his memoir, *WOW*.

My wings grew stronger during my stay as Writer in Residence at the Heinrich Böll Cottage in November 2009. When I was finally ready to admit that my work was worthy of publication, I tried a few publishers and dutifully filed away the polite rejections. I had no agent. Finally a proposal to Greenpoint

Press resulted in the birth of *Call of the Lark*. I chose the title because of a lark I heard in the garden of my childhood—the one I wrote about as a young nun when I was advised to nurture my writer's voice.

On May 10, 2012, the anniversary of my arrival in America fifty-four years earlier, the book was launched at the Irish Consulate in New York. I will always be grateful to Peter Ryan, who was then vice consul, for his generous support and for the celebration of this new phase of my life as a writer.

Traveling along the author's road, I'd heard that if you're really serious about putting the book in the hands of readers, you, the writer, have to do the legwork. I found this to be true and enjoyed the challenge of finding venues to read and share my work.

That summer, I took the book home to Aghamore. Local musician Joe Byrne collected a group of dancers, singers, and music makers to enhance the Mayo launch. My reading in the Kiltimagh local library brought together a lively book club, where I had the pleasure of meeting local writer Basil Burke. The Claremorris and Westport libraries also welcomed my request to host a local author.

In Gielty's pub during the Scoil Acla week that summer of 2012, it was thrilling to hear Macdara Woods, who helped me take my first steps as a writer, now introduce my book to an Achill audience. My teacher's remarks made me proud to realize how much I had grown since my first class, when he directed me to "listen to the silence."

Although promotion took time away from new writing, I began to realize that the challenge was worth the effort. It was obvious to me that this immigrant's journey from rural Mayo to the bustling city of fifties New York to leaving the world behind and then returning to build a new life had appeal to people not only of my own generation but others as well.

In writing *Call of the Lark*, I wanted to show that regardless of what road you take, you can always turn back and find a new path if you are determined to do so. I hoped also that my work would inspire and encourage other late bloomers who want to tell their own stories.

Finally, it was important for me to document the lives of a family named Mulligan who once lived in a thatched whitewashed cottage that stood in a field in the village of Caher, in the parish of Aghamore, in the County of Mayo, in the west of Ireland.

"The generation of Irish writers immediately before mine never allowed this burden to weigh them down. They learned to speak Irish, took their genetic purity for granted, and soldiered on. For us today the situation is more complex. We are more concerned with defining our Irishness than with pursuing it. We want to know what the word 'native' means, what the word 'foreign' means. We want to know if the words have any meaning at all. And persistent considerations like these erode old certainties and help clear the building site."

*Brian Friel*
*(9 January 1929–2 October 2015)*

# Kevin Holohan

Kevin Holohan was born in Dublin. He attended University College Dublin, studying Pure English. He spent six years teaching English as a foreign language in Castilla-La Mancha, Spain, where he learned to love Flamenco and eventually to read *Don Quixote* in the original. He moved to New York in 1996, where he lives with his wife and son. *The Brothers' Lot*, his first novel, was published by Akashic Books in 2011. He is currently working on his second novel.

# Standing in Doorways

[Long Pause.]

[Silence.]

[Throat clearing. Long silence. Shuffling of papers.]

*The Long-Suffering Reader*: Well? What's keeping you? What seems to be the delay here?

*The Self*: You'd think it would be easy, right? Write a few pages about being an Irish writer in New York. I am Irish and I write and I live in New York. Seems straightforward enough. But unfortunately it isn't that simple. Not for the likes of me. The only words in that second sentence I am sure of are *pages* and *New York; Irish* and *writer* are a bit more problematic.

*The Long-Suffering Reader*: Feck it, no! Is this going to be one of those ball-aching, hairsplitting essays all riddled with doubt and nit-picking?

*The Self*: I wouldn't go so far as to say riddled, but the answer is yes, a bit, so if that is going to get on your nerves, I would say cut your losses and move along now. You can leave me here to split hairs, pick nits, and gaze into my own navel in search of what *Irish* or *writer* means to me. Strange, isn't it, how introspection and rumination conjure such icky personal-grooming metaphors?

*The Long-Suffering Reader*: Ah, what the hell. I am here now and my bus is not due for another ten minutes, so you might as well get on with it. But leave the personal-grooming metaphors out of it, could you?

*The Self*: Fair enough, but we might have recourse to other metaphors as we go along.

*The Long-Suffering Reader*: That is acceptable. A question for you: Is this format you have us both stuck in now, this Mylesian dialogue, is this some kind of smart-alecky distancing device?

*The Self*: It is. Being a fiction writer, I am not entirely comfortable with talking about myself, so if you will indulge me in this, it would make it all a little easier on us both, I think. I can blame what I say on the questions you ask.

*The Long-Suffering Reader*: Reasonable gambit. I can't fault you for that. I am quite a shy sort myself too. So, what is so complicated about being Irish, then?

*The Self*: I am Irish, but perhaps what I don't understand is Brand Ireland and how it is supposed to inform my idea of self. The pressure to mistake mythologizing, public relations, and branding for identity can be very disconcerting.

When I first moved to New York, I had some Irish friends, here but I did not immediately gravitate towards any self-identified Irish or Irish-American community. It was all too easy to see only the green beer, shamrockery Irishness and dismiss it as kitsch. It has taken me a long time and a lot of wrangling to understand that in the often-unforgiving cauldron of jostling hyphenated American identities, there was little room for uncertainty or doubt. The post-colonial uncertainty, the jettisoning of valuable culture because it had been co-opted by church and state into de Valera's comely-maidens-dancing-at-crossroads mythology: that was the lot of many of my generation born in Ireland. Little of that is part of the story of Irish-American identity—one often predicated on leaving Ireland because of British misrule. A lot of recent emigration has been because of Irish, not British, misgovernment of Ireland. It may seem too churlish and ungrateful to Irish-Americans, but many of us did not feel exactly "cherished" by a nation for which emigration was the safety valve to ensure political stability. And so I inhabit a liminal space, long enough out of Ireland to have lost any instantaneous feel for the zeitgeist but not Irish-American, either. It can get drafty standing in the in-betweens, but I have learned to revalue much of the culture I had felt pushed away from. Time has divorced the culture from the bad old days of oppressive and repellent religious nationalism. But maybe we all worry too much about what being Irish means, anyway.

*The Long-Suffering Reader*: You hit on a thing there. You never seem to see French writers or Argentineans or Englishmen agonizing so much about what their adjective means, do you? Nice word that, *liminal*. Standing in the doorway. I will resist the temptation to make any cheap jokes about loitering in small-town drapers' doorways smoking Carrolls cigarettes and making snide comments about passers-by.

*The Self*: Your restraint is noted. And appreciated.

*The Long-Suffering Reader*: Right so. That's quite enough about Ireland to be going on with. How do you like New York, then?

*The Self*: Even at this early point in our acquaintance, would it surprise you at all to hear that I have mixed feelings?

*The Long-Suffering Reader*: It would not in the least surprise me. Is it your usual love/hate-the-place-you-have-to-live-every-day sort of thing? I feel that myself. You are a Dublin man, aren't you? I bet you had mixed feelings about there, too.

*The Self*: I did. I love Dublin. It is part of me, but it is too familiar, and there is something about me that needs to be out of my element to stay awake to things. New York is a hard city and so protean and ever-changing that it is unlikely to ever become my element, but it can be an exhilarating place. It is somewhat less vibrant since it became a place for the staggeringly and improbably wealthy to temporarily invest their surplus cash by buying apartments to leave empty, but it is still full of fascination.

*The Long-Suffering Reader*: Ah, don't start into that real-estate-bubble talk! Neither the time nor the place. Bonus points for *protean* there, by the way. Nice Joycean feel to it. So, Mr. Liminal Irishman, this writing thing? How overcomplicated can you possibly make that?

*The Self*: It's not so much the writing as the "writer" moniker.

*The Long-Suffering Reader*: For Christ's sake! Could you give me something solid to hold on to? Can you talk about writing for a little while? Do you use a computer at all?

*The Self*: I do. But I like pen and paper first.

*The Long-Suffering Reader*: There now. That wasn't hard, was it? See? We're making great strides. Another couple of well-aimed questions and we won't be able to shut you up about it. How did you start into this writing racket?

*The Self*: I have been writing since I was a teenager. I was in a garage band and started writing bad lyrics all full of mist and mountains and Orc-like demons, then graduated to writing bad poetry full of fog, coffee spoons, and sighs and broken hearts. I went to a poetry workshop in a basement on Frederick Street in Dublin one night when I was eighteen. The rest of them were a good bit older. They told me my poetry was derivative. Of course it was. I was eighteen. But it felt like a shitty thing to do to a kid so I never bothered going back.

The first book I remember reading and feeling almost from the first pages "I wish I had written this!" was Leonard Cohen's first novel, *Beautiful Losers*. Shortly thereafter I started a novel uncommonly like it in setting, theme, and style, which I thankfully abandoned and later lost. Not that I wish I had never done it. But it frightened me off novel writing for a long time. Everything is scaffolding. Juvenilia are embarrassing to look back on but absolutely essential to get through. I worry for young writers in MFA programs who feel they have to produce mature work or something that betrays its internal energy in order to look polished and mature. You have to make a mess and make mistakes.

*The Long-Suffering Reader*: How do you go about it? Are you a rise-before-dawn, five-hundred-words-a-day man?

*The Self*: I wish I was. I do like to work first thing in the morning before my head is awake enough to be censorious, but that rarely happens. Most of my writing time is actually spent walking and sifting and jotting stuff down, and only a small part of that ever gets to be part of anything. Another part of the time is spent transcribing these notes, draft texts on my phone, and voice mails I leave myself into a big composition book, and only a tiny portion of the time is spent at the desk in the cone of light trying to improve my atrocious typing. I wish I had a five-hundred-word-a-day habit, but I am terribly messy, inconsistent, and slow. [I'll vouch for that – Ed.]

It got to a point where I was so unsure if this was how writing was supposed to work that one day, five or six years ago, I stopped. Completely. Although I'd had some poems and short stories published, I was in one of those recurring I'll-never-be-published-because-everything-I-write-is-shite doldrums with my first novel. It was an identity experiment to see which was worse—being an office drone who scribbled with a drawerful of unpublishable half novels and stories, or just being an office drone and letting go of the whole writer thing altogether. It lasted a month. It felt really odd. It was like taking the lining out of a favorite coat. I did not know who I was or what to do with the world or the inside of my head. Then it became clear that whether or not anyone would ever publish or even read the scribbles, they were what made sense of things, a product of who I was and not something I just did. Jotting, scribbling, noting is my way to grab on to the world and put shape on it. If I never finish another thing, I will never stop writing, because I simply can't. I will always be running the voices through my inner ear to see what they say and where they might go.

*The Long-Suffering Reader*: So it must be very lucrative, then, this writing lark, if you are still doing it? Particularly in a pricey place like New York.

*The Self*: Yeah, right.

*The Long-Suffering Reader*: You have a day job of some sort, I take it?

*The Self*: I came to New York with a résumé that might as well have said: "B.A. in Anglo Saxon; six years teaching English as a foreign language in Spain; have seen spreadsheets." So I temped. That was what artsy types seemed to do. That or wait tables. I knew from past sorry experience that I had no aptitude for the hospitality industry. Temping was corporate America's unwitting funding of the arts. Expectations were low, so they gave you two days to finish a "project" that would take the moderately accomplished individual three hours. I learned to make my own stuff look vaguely like work on the screen, and got speedy with the ALT+TAB to throw up an array of worky-looking windows if anyone came too close. I think that influenced the way I write: short, typo-ridden bursts without ever looking back until I have a pile of tatters to assemble and clean. Over time some of the temp gigs began to have a corrosive effect. I reached a breaking point when I was in thrall on the trading floor at a large bank. I started working only at nonprofits. I had realized that if I wanted to do my own stuff, the day job could have nothing to do with writing. It was never a conscious strategy; it was something I stumbled into. Others make different arrangements and teach or edit or write for magazines with real deadlines—a thing I could never do. I now have a grown-up day job that matters to me, involving sifting numbers and data for a nonprofit humanitarian organization. It's not heroic work, but the widgets at the end of it do good and save kids' lives, so I can sleep at night. The day job occupies one side of my brain and I try to use the other side to scribble at the weekends or very early in the mornings.

Most of the time, the two manage to play quite nicely together. That is not to say that a Medici-sized endowment to further my scribbling endeavors would not be welcomed, but it is not expected.

*The Long-Suffering Reader*: How was it to get your first book published?

*The Self*: It was thrilling. I'd had several long, fruitless campaigns of trying to sell *The Brother's Lot* to agents that elicited a lot of "really-love-this-but-have-no-idea-how-to-sell-it" responses. I knew Johnny Temple at Akashic Books and asked him to look at the query letter and synopsis I was using to see if there was something that was potentially scary to agents or publishers. One of their managing editors happened to be living in Ireland at the time, and she asked to see the manuscript. I was excited but worked to keep my expectations realistic. The editorial board talked amongst themselves for six months and then offered to publish it. I was thrilled. They had a great reputation among independent presses for integrity and fairness. The editing process was a tremendous experience. Their editorial suggestions demonstrated that they understood what the book was trying to be and showed me where I was getting in my own way. I learned a great deal about storytelling.

I was never comfortable saying I am a writer until I became an author, having come embarrassingly late to the understanding that an author is one who has been published and a writer is one who writes. Somehow when I was growing up in Dublin, these terms were interchangeable, and to say I am a writer was a lofty claim that would be immediately met with an "Oh, yeah? And what have you published?" In the Dublin of my making, "writer" was not an aspiration or a vocation but a judgment conferred by others.

Being published is an encouraging external approval. It has also put me in the company of others engaged in the racket of writing, to compare doubts, fears, aspirations, inspirations, little triumphs, approaches to work, approaches to unwork, and to find some solace in the realization that, ISBN or no, we all share the same compulsive need to put things down on paper.

*The Long-Suffering Reader*: That seems to be working out for you, then. Are you working on a new novel?

*The Self*: I am. It's...

*The Long-Suffering Reader*: Uh-oh. Here's me bus. Good luck now!

[Exit in omnibus.]

*The Self*: All the best. Safe home. I'll tell you about the new book another time.

JP Donleavy with the director Philip Wiseman, center, and Brendan Behan,

# J.P. Donleavy

*(April 23, 1926–September 11, 2017)*

There is a long history of Irish writers fleeing their native land for foreign shores. J.P. Dunleavy was one of those rare Irish writers who started out on the western side of the Atlantic, in America, and moved back to Ireland, like a wild salmon swimming upstream in search of the source.

James Patrick Donleavy was born in Brooklyn on April 23, 1926, to Irish immigrant parents, Patrick, from Longford, and Margaret, from Galway. When James was still a child, the family moved to the Bronx, where he was raised in a house on West 238th Street, just a few blocks from the Woodlawn Cemetery. In a *Paris Review* interview in 1975, Donleavy referred to the Woodlawn Cemetery as "the most peaceful place in America." He spent much time contemplating there while working on his most famous book, *The Ginger Man.*

As a boy, James was a restless student, spending most of

his education being shifted from one school to another. He attended Saint Barnabas in Woodlawn, Fordham Preparatory School, Roosevelt High School in Yonkers, and the Manhattan Preparatory School. As a teenager, he also frequented the New York Athletic Club and tried his hand at amateur boxing.

After two years in the Navy, from 1944 to 1946, he received an honorable discharge and headed to Dublin to attend Trinity College on the GI Bill.

He didn't start out as a writer, though. In Dublin, Donleavy spent his time studying art and painting. He managed to mount a few minor art shows, but realized quickly that his artwork was not the path to financial independence. In 1949, he quit Trinity without a degree and began working in earnest on a novel.

In a strange twist of fate, he would cross paths with the writer Brendan Behan in a pub. Behan insulted Donleavy right out of the gate by calling him a narrowback (a derogatory term for an Irish-American). The two men took to the street to box it out, but Behan decided the better of it and talked Donleavy out of it. They went back to their drinks and became fast friends.

While Donleavy was out of town on a trip shortly afterward, Behan broke into his house in a drunken stupor, and found and read the manuscript of his novel in progress, *The Ginger Man*. Behan was even so bold as to scribble editing notes throughout the pages and sign his name to it...before stealing all Donleavy's shoes.

Frustrated with work on the book, Donleavy returned to his mother's house in Woodlawn to try and complete it there. In 1952, he submitted the finished manuscript to Scribner's, who rejected it because of its obscene content.

Back in Ireland in 1954, Behan suggested he send it to Olympia Press in Paris, which had published *Lolita*. Olympia loved the book and agreed to print it right away, but, much to Donleavy's further frustration, Olympia published the novel as pornography. It was an association Donleavy tried desperately to distance himself from. (The subsequent legal battle would drag on for twenty years and culminate in a final stroke of genius by Donleavy when he sent his wife to buy the press out from under the unsuspecting owner using her name.)

By 1955, *The Ginger Man* had the dubious distinction of being banned in both Ireland and the United States. It was a bit of profound good fortune for Donleavy. The more press the obscenity changes garnered, the greater the demand for the book. The reading public were driven out of morbid curiosity to discover the antics of the novel's scoundrel protagonist, Sebastian Dangerfield.

In the years since, *The Ginger Man* has been granted a place on the Modern Library's 100 Best Novels list and is estimated to have sold upwards of 45 million copies worldwide to date.

The financial success of the novel allowed Donleavy to buy a 260-year-old estate outside of Mullingar, Westmeath, where he continued to write for another 45 years.

He also went back to painting and has had roughly twenty gallery shows of his work in Dublin, London, and New York.

In the past decade, the actor Johnny Depp visited Donleavy in Mullingar, where they discussed the possibility of finally bringing Sebastian Dangerfield to the big screen. Singer Shane MacGowan, who famously named one of his best-known songs for the title of a Donleavy novel, *A Fairy Tale of New York*, has been approached to appear in the movie.

J.P. Dunleavy died in a hospital in Mullingar of an apparent stoke, on September 11 2017.

Colin Broderick

# Kevin Fortuna

Born in 1971 in Georgetown, Kevin Fortuna grew up in Atlantic City, New York and New Orleans, and was educated at Georgetown and the University of New Orleans. He's an entrepreneur, author and filmmaker whose family hails from Cobh, County Cork. His critically acclaimed story collection, *The Dunning Man*, was the basis of the film of the same name which released in 2016. He is currently at work on his second film, *Flogging Maggie*.

# Jimmy's Whip

My last name isn't Irish but it's lucky.

I'm Irish on my mom's side and my dad was full-blown Italian, the son of a cobbler. My last name, Fortuna, translated literally from the Italian means "fortune"—which is neither good luck nor bad. I've had my share of both. But thanks to my Irish roots and my decision to move to New York, it's mostly the good kind.

My uncle Jimmy Ellis, on my mother's side, made his living as a harbor pilot in Cobh, County Cork, Ireland, the last port of call for the *Titanic* at a time when the waterside village was still called Queenstown under British rule. The *Titanic* never made it to New York, but many of Jimmy's relatives did. Those people flung themselves across the Atlantic, riding on a War Bride's ship after World War I and later in steerage in the *QE2*.

Jimmy stayed and kept on guiding ships into Cobh Harbor until he retired more than a decade ago. And my time with Jimmy was an indelible part of my first trip to Ireland. Jimmy was our blood connection to the place and people. I was college-aged, slogging through my extended adolescence and accompanied by my two brothers. I was too much of a punk to fully appreciate what Jimmy showed us. It was more show than tell. Jimmy didn't say much—and he still doesn't. I can remember sitting in the kitchen of his townhome, my Aunt Olive fussing about the kitchen, overcooking the potatoes and meat, and Jimmy sitting in his armchair, sipping gin from a tall glass with his massive etymological dictionary on the table by his side. For Jimmy's job, the house was wired with a dedicated line tied to a phone that rang so loudly it could wake the dead. When fog covered the majestic Cobh Harbor, preventing the lighthouse from serving its purpose, that phone summoned Jimmy to the harbor, to the rescue.

Our first night in Cobh, the harbor bat phone didn't ring. We sat around and drank and listened to Olive's stories about the family we never knew. Friends and distant cousins came to the house to visit with us. At first, my brothers and I tried to hide from the company. Such was our habit at family gatherings of any kind. Random cousins by the dozens, Irish and Italian, whom we'd see every few years when someone got baptized or buried... who could be bothered? Plus, on that trip to Cobh, we were scared. As scared as Uncle Jimmy was of the spicy Italian sausage my brother Joey had brought in from New York City. We were unaccustomed to the kind of social grace and hospitality that was second nature to our Irish relatives, and it was too much for us. But Olive shamed us up from our hiding place in the basement and into small talk with the visitors with funny accents. I don't remember what everyone talked about, but I do remember lots of questions about America, and I remember Jimmy in that chair in the corner, observing and holding court in his reticent way, his hand resting on that big, well-thumbed dictionary. From time to time, a patch of conversation would make him open his tome and his mouth. He'd join the conversation by explaining the Latinate (or other) root history of a word used by his guests. This is Jimmy's conversational style, his way into the easy Blarney patois, his thing. He finds moments that give him an opportunity to explain the birth and winding staircase of words, the building blocks of history and culture. He does it in the way a priest might explain the sacraments or a carpenter might explain the building materials and the proper way to swing a hammer or sand a floor. Language for Jimmy is a mystical thing, the pneuma of our race. Words are like the Irish dirt beneath him—sacred and cherished. And he speaks so little that everyone hangs on his precisely chosen words whenever he looks up over his bifocals and finally offers them up.

Back then, even in my disaffected Salinger state of mind, the poetry of that first visit with Jimmy, the continuum of the writer's DNA in our family, moved me and lit some kind of fire in my gut—or, more precisely, an insatiable hunger. Some switch within me flipped, made me hungry for the truth. The alchemic continuum of my Irish blood became manifest: my uncle Jimmy Ellis, the scholar and seaman, has a very true love, bordering on obsession, for language. He has his whip, his lion-taming control over the fierce superpower of words as the living and breathing history and heatmap of art and culture and wit.

That's my Irish inheritance: Jimmy's Whip.

We Fortunas got Jimmy's whip.

My brother Joey, our "native" guide on this trip to our homeland, was living and working in Dublin, paying his bills gigging as a musician and writing as a stringer for *the The Irish Times* and *Irish Independent* and various other Irish publications. Joey always wanted to be a writer and a rock star, and he was living his dream. My older brother and I have always been best friends and each other's role models by turns, driven to achieve by a healthy sibling rivalry peppered with professional and creative collaboration and bare-knuckle boxing and put-out-yer-eye BB-gun fights and vandalism and shoplifting and various other acts of youthful indiscretion. On that first trip to Ireland, I realized the extent of Joey's success as a writer and a musician. By then, Joey had published multiple short stories and dozens of articles, and he had performed with his rock band on RTE (Irish national television) on a show called *Zig and Zag* (kind of like Ireland's Muppet version of *Good Morning America*).

And I thought this: If Joey can do this fun shit, then so can I. And I set my mind to plot a course to catch up with and outdo him (as brothers do).

I started writing fiction and reading the authors I brought home from Ireland: Patrick McCabe, Roddy Doyle, John McGahern. I decided to turn down the beaten path to take a full ride to study fiction at the University of New Orleans.

Only to learn that the writer's life can be a shitshow of solitude and poverty and selfishness and narcissistic pretension, so...

About a year later, I had ditched the starving artist thing and needed a stopgap before getting back on the capitalist train that would ultimately relocate me to Manhattan and a career in the internet space.

So I was back shining shoes and working the counter at Fortuna's Shoe Repair, the company my dad's father had started in 1943, the business that paid most of our family's bills. Ironically, the going concern business of Fortuna's was now run by my Irish mother who has more business sense in her pinky than my dad, the good doctor, had in his whole brain and body.

My siblings and I all worked at the shop while growing up, so it was nice to be back, if even for a little while. At Fortuna's, I was surrounded by immigrants from all over the globe—Latin America, Vietnam, Russia, Italy and African Americans from D.C. and other southern cities. These men (and they were *all* men) were like uncles to me. They taught me the value of focus and craft. They taught me how to drink and talk to girls and to shoot pool. Cool footnote: my first pool cue was fashioned from a broomstick on my grandfather's shoe-sanding machines by one Pete Martin, convicted murderer and one-time member of Jackie Wilson's entourage who worked for Fortuna's until the week before he died. (Pete was always quick to point out that the murder was an accident... he was aiming for his wife but shot his sister-in-law instead... missed his target. My grandfather sponsored his work-release parole from prison and let him live in the shop on Wisconsin Avenue until he got on his feet.) In spite of the hell he'd survived, Pete Martin had a permanent smile and an ironic, devastating wit—never failing to find a way to laugh and make fun.

Pete and the other men at the shop were, in many ways, like me and my siblings. Fishes out of water. We were shanty striving progeny of recent immigrants penetrating the insular barbed-wired-up clubs of privilege and wealth, trying to make a better life. They worked long, hard hours and toiled (mostly) without complaint.

My Irish mother worked as hard as any of them, and she mothered and protected her staff. Mom spent money we didn't have to sponsor work visas and pay rent and Catholic school tuition, including ours. My father was a great doctor and a decent man, but he was god awful with money. His failure to build financial security for us was directly tied to his unwillingness to ever turn away an uninsured patient in the many emergency rooms he built and ran. Dad pissed away everything he made on doomed investments and left mom holding the bag and the reins and the fate of our education.

My mother became our family's main provider, the wise, fierce matriarch, the stoical captain of our ship on a raging sea. Our harbor pilot.


There's a shoe box in my house filled with handwritten letters from my brother Joey, sent from his cold-water flat on Lower Gardiner Street in Dublin. Every letter has the same greeting, invented by me and adopted by Joey, at the start of this pre-email pen-pal exchange: "I hope this finds you well and that you are not bored by the days ahead...." Some of these letters make me wince, but some of them make me very proud of that box of brotherly love. Those letters contain true (and sometimes smart) words and about life and art and culture and girls and boys and the batshit-crazy stuff happening around us. We wrote about hopes and dreams, about striving and struggling for meaning and trying to make a difference in a bent world. And in one of those letters, I made a promise to Joey that I'd try to write for a living for one simple reason: It was the one and only job I could imagine doing for the rest of my life without getting bored. I had exemplars like William Trevor and John McGahern and the greats—Fitzgerald and Hemingway, Dostoyevskey and Joyce. And Shane MacGowan.

My return to Fortuna's was short-lived. I'd soon find myself in New York City, working in the tech industry, trying to make good on the pricey undergrad degree I'd earned.

That was more than 20 years ago, and I've never left NYC.

Along the way, thanks to the help of good friends, I got the opportunity to finish my MFA at the University of New Orleans through its low-residency program. That led to the publication of my first book, *The Dunning Man*, a collection of short stories that led to my first independent film by the same name. I'm now making my second film, based on another story from that book.

But I'm not quitting my day job. Turns out that, here in NYC, I found another job I can do for a long while without getting bored. Building tech companies has been a fun ride and now I'm helping to run a collective of tech startups called Gramercy Labs, just off Times Square.

Building internet companies is a lot like fiction writing: You need to tell a good story. You need art and science and pattern recognition and synthesis. You need to understand characters and treat them with empathy. You need to trust your gut and take big risks on people.

Gramercy Labs has had a diverse mix of talent and people: Actors, musicians, and even a professional poker player. A girl from Eastern Europe who stabbed her father to prevent the murder of her mother and had to be airlifted out to NYC, the son of a forklift operator, an underground hip-hop guy who worked as a home-health-care worker before coming to Gramercy, a former janitor now lead editor for one of my media sites. The son of a brilliant immigrant from India, a structural engineer, who cut through the barbed wire and rose from managing laundromats to his position as the head structural engineer of the MTA, a whip-smart Jewish girl from Long Island by the name of Sales, anglicised from "Zales" to dodge the anti-semitism that still plagues our land of the free. Scrappers, sons and daughters of immigrants, part of the New York City tribe sailing here for a better life. These people make the most of the opportunity in front of them. They bring the hunger.

Rewind back to that first trip to Ireland, to Cobh. On our last full day with Jimmy Ellis, he announced that we were going for "a bit of a hike." He wanted to show us something. Jimmy drove down a narrow one-lane road through fog and bramble. Eventually he parked the car and we walked off the road. An hour later, we were cutting through the thick woods outside of the village, breathing in the wet, dirt-soaked Irish air. We had no idea what Jimmy wanted to show us. We didn't ask, and Jimmy didn't tell. We walked in silence through bog and woods until we came upon a black cylindrical thing that looked like it had grown right up out of the ground. The forest had almost swallowed it, but we could tell that others had come before us and wiped away the weeds and mud to have a better look, to lay hands on it. We walked up to it and touched it and realized it was black and metal, cast iron, and covered with a thick film of rust. As I touched it and ran my hand along its surface, the hair on the back of my neck stood up. I couldn't say why, but I knew immediately that this thing held some kind of talismanic power.

Jimmy stopped and said, "There it is, lads. That's a famine pot. That's where your great-grandparents were fed by the

British."

Another part of our Irish inheritance: *the hunger*. Hunger for knowledge and experience and accomplishment and a life that gives us stories worth telling. And for some way to tell those stories.

Jimmy's Whip.

# Christopher John Campion

Christopher John Campion grew up Irish American on Long Island and is the author of the recovery memoir *Escape From Bellevue: A Dive Bar Odyssey*. He is a singer-songwriter-troubadour by trade who puts out records and performs over 200 shows a year in tri-state area bars, rock clubs, and canteens—telling stories and singing songs. In addition Mr. Campion regularly writes for the newspaper *The East Hampton Star* and is currently at work on a new monologue-music piece. He lives in Queens with his wife Chrisie.

# Watch the Gap

I'm gonna start off by telling you what I consider to be the most poignant and pivotal moment I've had as a writer living in New York City.

My wife, Chrisie, and I were downtown slushing through the dark gray gruel of a two-days dirty snowstorm and being weighed down by some dense municipal folders we were carrying. Contained within these manila monstrosities were thick informational booklets, civic disclaimers, invasive questionnaires, and myriad pages of a paper chase that I really wasn't looking forward to acquainting myself with once we got home. These folders were seriously heavy—made more cumbersome by the fact that they were soaking wet with my failure. The paperwork was applications for food stamps.

We made the turn onto Sixth Avenue and began walking with an even greater sense of purpose for fear of running into anyone we knew from the neighborhood and having to explain where we were coming from and what we were carrying—the standard salvo of innocuous interrogation that comes with any sidewalk stop-'n'-chat. You can tell yourself anything you want so as not to feel the shame of going on public assistance, and we did. "We're artists…sometimes you just have to go on the dole, luv," I said to Chrisie with a half smile, dialing up an English accent in an attempt to make it cool. It didn't—we still felt like losers.

Just then we passed a Barnes & Noble store, looked up, and saw, prominently displayed in the window in a fateful act of karmic mockery, the paperback edition of my book, *Escape from Bellevue*, which had been published only the year before in hardcover by Gotham Books. Oh, how the mighty had fallen. Well, maybe not mighty so much as "thought I had a good shot."

I conjured the most rubbery, wide-eyed Rodney Dangerfield face I could, then struck a celebratory Heisman pose in front of the window, tucking the welfare folder under one arm like a football and thrusting the other triumphantly skyward, defiantly straight-arming God. Chrisie took a quick snap and we laughed. If my years in New York have taught me anything, it's that there's always a good joke lying next to you at rock bottom if you're willing to spring out of the fetal position and claim it.

Don't get me wrong—it's not that I wasn't selling any books. I was…lots of 'em, in fact…to the Strand Bookstore. We'd been making runs over there all week, literally looting every last title from the shelves of our apartment just to be able to eat that day. Anything in reasonable condition with a sturdy binder that might fetch us some cash went. Tragically, the cookbooks sold for the most money.

One fervent foodie even bought one right out of my hand while I was standing on the bartering line. Guess he figured he'd get a better number from me than them. the furtive little fucker. As we were making the exchange, he delightedly said, "This is kismet…I've been thinking a lot lately about taking up French cooking." A response quickly formed in my head…*Yeah, well, I hope you choke on your first batch of crepes, my frog-ophile friend* but, sent through my filter, just came out, "Enjoy." That's New York for you right there; even a used cookbook and someone is chompin' at your ankles hustling for a better deal.

How did I go so broke inside only a year? Well, in New York it's pretty easy. Money evaporates out of your pocket just walking down the street here. Most of us are just one financial setback away from total ruin in any given year. Mine was more of a misstep, abiding obsequiously by the notion that in order to sell my book, I had to focus on that and only that, therefore living off my advance and ignoring all other means of income.

As a musician/singer/wiseass-on-a-microphone by trade,

that meant throwing over my real paying gigs, which barely got me by to begin with, for free events in bookstores and spending all my waking hours dreaming up Internet promotions and producing videos in the hopes they'd "go viral," an expression I can't fuckin' stand to this day. I rationalized solely stumping for the book as "investing in myself"…a terrible idea. Of course you should always try to sell your wares and be fastidious in your efforts, but to do so and not cover your ass, in this town? Certifiably stupid is all I can say.

Most other writers are professors or journos or have real jobs—some fortification against being put out onto the street if their books don't sell. My life had never even resembled that. I had been walking a tightrope without a net in the West Village for eighteen years, living by any means necessary, never having any savings, hand-to-mouth always, and my day of reckoning had finally come.

Greenwich Village was still affordable for artists when I moved in back in the summer of '93, and there were even some surviving members of the Beats still around. I remember drinking in the afternoon in a bar called the Lion's Head, a reputed watering hole for authors and crusty old newspapermen. I was nursing a pint and reading a book of poems called *Gasoline,* written by Gregory Corso. I'd picked it up because I'd heard that Bob Dylan had been really taken with it before he wrote all those great songs in the early to mid-sixties, so I sought it out.

The bartender, a big square-jawed guy with graying temples, put his elbow down in front of me and asked, "Like that book, do ya?" I said, "Yeah…really brilliant stuff…I love this guy!" He started washing out a glass and with an impish grin motioned toward an old man napping at the other end of the bar and said, "Well why don't you go down there and tell him how much?" Didn't have the balls to do it and to this day still not sure if the man pouring wasn't winding me up, but I like to believe it was him. People said he used to go there.

The Village of my undoing in this, the year 2011, looked nothing like that. Places like the Lion's Head and a lot of other cool canteens and gin mills I had played music in for years were now gone, and so were all the artists. Rents had soared and eviscerated the bohemian vibe and replaced it with a new homogenized, manicured, and semi-suburban way of life. Baby strollers, Jamba juice, fancy restaurants, and Starbucks were now the order of the day, and in the evenings the sidewalks would fill up four across with high-heeled, tipsy, shrilly throngs of women in their early twenties who I suspected had watched too much *Sex and the City* and were now determined to live out the show's precepts in a cosmo-consuming hookup haze in the Meatpacking District.

With this newfound encroachment, my subsequent curmudgeonly rage, and an inability to pay the ever steep and inclining rent, I decided to employ the advice I'd remembered from an old Driver's Ed manual that read, "When the car is skidding, the only way to right the vehicle and come to a full stop is to turn into it." Translation: rather than claw our way to eventually squaring the back rent with the landlord, an implausible ideation given my current income anyway, we instead allowed ourselves to be unceremoniously bounced from the premises.

Pretty humiliating even after you decide to fold and know it's coming, what with the all-too-eager-to-be-obnoxious paper servers persistently knocking at your door and eviction notices waiting for you when you got home that all your neighbors had already seen. Then when they'd run into you in the hall, they'd avoid eye contact, maybe so as not to embarrass you but also maybe so as not to get any of your misbegotten mojo on them through incidental contact. No one wants to stand next to the guy who just rolled craps.

So to the outer boroughs we went, searching for an affordable solution, but on our meager budget we were still looking at pretty slim pickin's, mostly falling-down cold-water flats in high-crime areas. We almost pulled the trigger on one that would've been a pretty harsh existence, when out of left field and well into the eleventh hour my cousin George swooped down to our rescue, wrangling us a nice one-bedroom in his building in the land of my forebears, the Irish blue-collar burg of Woodside, Queens.

Both sides of my family had settled in Woodside after coming over here from Ireland in the latter part of the nineteenth century and doing post-Ellis Island stints in Lower Manhattan—so in a weird way I was simply following the old family-migration blueprint. My folks had both grown up there, met, married, and started raising a family, and just before I was born, moved us all out to Long Island, where there would be more room for a family of eight.

Growing up, we would come back to Woodside often for weddings and wakes (same amount of drinking—almost identical occasions by midnight to a child's eye), visiting grandparents, and family reunions, with all my aunts, uncles, and cousins—so I knew the neighborhood well but never intimately.

Manhattan is the Mecca, it's the summit, the Rome of the Roman Empire, and where most everyone who wants to succeed in art, fashion, or business wants to live—or so it would seem. It had very much been that for me. Whenever I was out of town and people asked me where I lived, I was proud to say, "Manhattan." It meant I was part of it...in the game...playing to win! Now, this living in Queens thing...I don't know. I just felt beaten, like I'd been sent down to the minors.

On moving day, Chrisie and I sent the last of our things on

ahead and were riding out to our new life in Queens on the 7 train. When we stepped off at our stop, I noticed the sign "Watch the Gap." It resonated instantly. It felt like Neil Armstrong's "one giant step" in reverse. It also seemed like that warning had come too late…that I was already in the gap…that I hadn't fuckin' watched it! I wasn't writing anything new, bereft of the belief that anything I created could work, and was pretty much just passing the days wallowing in self-pity.

We got up into the new apartment and, not wanting to deal with it yet, I shot right out to the supermarket on the corner to pick up some essentials. While there, I decided to grab us some sandwiches and stood in line at the deli counter behind this slovenly fat guy in an oversized green Jets sweatshirt. He barked at the teenage clerk, "Uhhhh, yeah…I'll have a halfa pounda baloney."

This was a little bit exciting to me—almost twenty years in Manhattan and not once had I witnessed anyone ordering cold cuts. The clerk weighed it and handed it to him. The guy looked at me incredulously, bouncing the baloney up and down in his hand, then switching to his other hand and doing the same thing, figuring his own calculation as to the weight of it, then pointedly asked the clerk, "This HALFA POUND?" Clerk nodded yes.

My man started backpedaling away, still bouncing it in his hand, and, as if to send the clerk a clear and intimidating message not to dare try shorting him any baloney in the future, says, "Yeah…well…feels a little light…is all I'm sayin'." So Queens was this. The kid had put it on a digital scale, but that's beside the point, I guess. The point is that in that instant, after shaking my head and laughing my ass off, I fell in love with the neighborhood and knew I was home. I can't explain it—I was just ready to be there.

It occurred to me that it matters not where you live but what you do. I also realized that one of my biggest mistakes was that

I'd always been too myopic about Manhattan, never venturing out to do anything anywhere else. So I developed a new strategy and began booking shows in all five boroughs and beyond, eventually covering the whole tri-state area and, in turn, getting back to sea level financially.

This gave way to some new inspiration. Turns out traveling back from a gig in the bowels of the New York City transit system at three in the morning, you get to see some pretty cosmic shit. It's a candy store of wanton chaos for any writer, and bringing this all down to date, I have collected quite a few hair-raising tales and am currently assembling them for my new joint.

I also started writing songs and releasing records again. In all my years living in the city, I've never felt like more of a New Yorker, because now I see every corner and every curb. All socioeconomic rungs of the ladder are represented on my schedule, from hoity-toity events in the Hamptons to a beloved bar I regularly play in Sunset Park, Brooklyn, directly across the street from a gangland headquarters. "Yale to jail"—I play 'em all.

Most of my nights end with me riding home with my fellow exhausted night workers, mining my imagination for an idea or just looking out the window...watching the traffic flow... lurching ever slow...through the great borough...of Queens... on the 7 train.

7 Train in Veins....
*The 7 train is in my veins, it carries me home through my pain....*
*and is the place where my thoughts graze...*
*These days I'm a monkey in the middle*
*with a heartache from an ancient Irish fiddle*
*Feelin' hum drum like that bum*
*out on the sidewalk where he sits...*
*takin' big sips...*
*thumbin' his nose at the apocalypse....*

"Being Irish was the only thing I couldn't resign from. I stopped being a Catholic and I stopped being a Democrat."

*William Kennedy*

*(Born January 16, 1928)*

# Dennis Driscoll

Dennis Driscoll grew up Irish-American in the upper reaches of Manhattan in a neighborhood called Inwood, alongside poet Jim Carroll. Driscoll has toured with the legendary American rock band Television and travels to Ireland on a regular basis to perform with Glen Hansard. His most recent collection, *Inwood Stories,* was recorded in 2011.

# When Inwood Was Irish

I grew up in a predominantly Irish-American neighborhood called Inwood, in the extreme northern part of Manhattan. Lots of socializing went on in the 116 bars and taverns that dotted the neighborhood. Along with drink, these places provided conversation. The reason people went to them was the company they provided. Before we were legally permitted to enter bars, we met in the park and drank. The best part of drinking with friends was that many of us had a way with words. We'd form what we called the vicious circle and either tell stories or make fun of each other or both. I know the Irish are known for their storytelling ability and the oral tradition. I don't know if it was genetically passed on, but there were many of us in Inwood who were good at telling stories. I wrote a little bit in school and had less of a problem when it came to creative writing than math or science. I had aspirations of being a lawyer.

All that changed when I was fourteen years old. That was the year I discovered drugs. Most of us started drinking and some messed with glue at the age of twelve. I was one of those kids who tried glue. I found out what it was like to get high on alcohol, and enjoyed the effects but didn't particularly like the act of drinking all that liquid. Glue was a good alternative to drinking but not socially acceptable; no one seemed bothered by twelve-year-old kids drinking. So glue broke down some barriers as to what was acceptable to me. Glue was a good escape from worries about school, a little vacation in two number-2 bags.

So when pot became popular, I didn't have the hang-ups some kids had about smoking the evil weed. Before I left grammar school, I had smoked my first joint. By June, right after graduating, I took LSD for the first time. It was a blue pill called Blue Cheer, named after the hard-rock band Blue Cheer, and made by the most famous acid chemist, Owsley Stanley. Doses were high and the acid was "clean." I knew before long that heroin was in my future. Heroin was becoming very popular amongst kids my age. One or two of my friends had been using it for up to a year, and I just knew I'd like it. Speed was never very popular with most of the kids using heroin. I did go through a period in my school days where I would steal my mother's Dexedrine diet pills, which seemed to be great for writing assignments in school until you reread the required three-paragraph compositions that turned into six pages of repeated regurgitated garbage.

Gradually heroin started to take over more and more of my life. Before heroin, I had been interested in playing bass guitar, but that faded as the drug use increased. By age sixteen, the heroin was taking physical control of me, giving me withdrawal symptoms unless I provided my body with the drug. I found ways to get money for drugs, which usually entailed stealing and usually from my family or my job at the Grand Union grocery store. But heroin was cheap back then, and it took me two years to get my first habit, so if I didn't have money, I just didn't get high.

By the age of nineteen, it was getting bad. My parents had had enough, knowing I was a junkie but hoping I'd clean up. Finally I was told to leave my family's home. By this time, we lived in the Bronx and I had nowhere in Inwood to go. I ended up on Twelfth Street with my friends, a local Inwood couple who moved out of the hood to the East Village. The East Village always had an attraction to kids into drugs, sex, and rock 'n' roll. We'd take the A train from the first stop in Inwood, 207th Street, to West Fourth Street, and walk through Greenwich Village to the East Village and the Fillmore East. I lived with my friends on Twelfth Street for about as long as it took me to kick my habit. I then called my parents and agreed to get on a methadone program if they would let me come home.

I got on a program on the Upper East Side, which my parents paid for, which was the home to many well-off junkies. Eventually I moved to a city-run program and spent a lot of time working crap jobs. I started messing around a bit and stole some cash from my parents, and once again it was time to go. This time it was for good. I split an apartment with an older guy who had been to Vietnam and wasn't really easy to live with. He was constantly stealing my weed and just not being very fun to live with, and he probably felt the same way about me, but at least I never stole from him.

It was then I got my own place and started playing bass guitar. The methadone gave me time to live without the worry of needing a fix. I started to live a semi-normal life. I read a lot, mainly biographies and true crime and historical books. Lots of counterculture books.

Books by black revolutionaries and hippies like Abbie Hoffman and Jerry Rubin and my favorite Irish author, Brendan Behan. At the end of the seventies, I started playing in bands in the East Village and hung out with lots of creative people, frequenting CBGB's and Max's Kansas City, eventually playing in both of those clubs.

I started to wean myself from methadone, a long, slow process if you wanted to stay clean.

About this time a new author caught my eye. He was also writing music and started a band on the West Coast called the Jim Carroll Band. I got his book *The Basketball Diaries* and soon realized I knew this guy. He was an Inwood guy, a guy who wrote poetry and played amazing basketball until the drugs took hold. I read the book and realized most of the people mentioned in the book and in his hit song "People Who Died" were people I knew, though with changed names of nicknames. This book was an inspiration, and his popularity was encouraging, knowing that people were interested in the life of a thirteen-year-old junkie poet.

I tried writing songs around this time and never was able to finish one. I didn't really consider myself a poet but more of a musician. I felt very comfortable onstage with a band and really enjoyed it, but eventually my band broke up, and I joined several others, but none of them really went anywhere. Being on the Lower East Side reintroduced me to my old friend heroin. In the media, there was all this talk about the new, much stronger heroin on the streets, and the LES was the center of the most outrageous outdoor drug markets—lines of junkies up to a block long waiting to see the man. I never allowed myself to get as strung out as before, but I needed out of the East Village for a while.

I moved back to Inwood and got a straight job at Citibank. I'm not really a nine-to-five guy, though. I did that for a number of years and eventually left for another shot at music, ending up in San Francisco playing in an African rock band. After a couple of years, it was back to my beloved Inwood, always my home.

An opportunity arose when my brother and some friends of mine opened a restaurant on Twelfth Street, the same street I'd ended up on twenty years before. Owning a restaurant was more my style, and I worked on the books there. The best part of owning a restaurant is having a place to invite your friends for a meal. After a couple of years, the restaurant got pretty popular. One day an old friend of mine, Frank Murray, who managed the Pogues at their peak, called me and told me he was bringing in a new band he was managing, an Irish band. He told me where they were playing, and I went to see them and loved the music. I loved the band members' enthusiasm and energy. These kids were not jaded, loved what they were doing, and did it well. The lead singer/songwriter was a guy named Glen Hansard. He had been busking and making a living playing music since he was thirteen. He ended up in a film called *The Commitments,* and with the money and fame he earned from the film, he started the band the Frames, who I met in New York. Glen and I hit it off, and when the band left town, Glen, who loved New York, stayed for a few days longer. I called him up to see what he was doing and asked him if he was hungry. He said yes, he and his friend were hungry but had no money at all. I said, "Glen, I asked if you were hungry!" and he said yes and I said come down to the restaurant. We stayed in touch whenever he was in New York.

Not long after, I started doing inventory on Sundays at the restaurant with my partner Steve. Seemed like every Sunday, I'd end up telling him a new story. After a while, he suggested I start writing them down and we could put them on a website for the restaurant. However, after some thought, we came to the conclusion that my stories were not going to be something that would entice people to come to the place, so the site didn't happen. But I did write the stories down. I had no idea what to do with them, but I kept writing, eventually emailing them to my Irish friend Glen. He seemed to love my stories and would write me back and encourage me to keep writing.

In 1999, I visited Dublin for the first time, staying with another Irish musician, Mic Christopher, a great songwriter and all-around great guy. During my visit, Glen came over to say hello—all of Dublin's buskers and street musicians used to drop by Mic's house for a cup of tea. Glen informed me he had a solo gig at a local club, Whelan's, and asked me if I would open the show for him. I was pretty surprised. I had no idea what he wanted me to do. He told me to read one of my stories and he would back me up musically. I was kind of shocked. I really had no intention of doing anything with my writing. I called my dad and told him, "They want me to read my stories here onstage," He said, "You don't live there—if you suck, get out of town!" That seemed like good advice, and I did the show. It was a sold-

167

out show, and I'd never read in public. Playing bass in a band is a breeze compared to getting on stage and baring your soul. I ended up doing another show in Dublin before I went home, and started to think that maybe I was on to something here. Glen continued to support me and got me to go to Ireland and do shows with him and the Frames.

When I got back to New York, I started doing readings at my restaurant, always with different local musicians backing me up. I still had no idea of what to do with my stories. How to get them published, how to get them heard. As time passed, I started recording vocals with my friend Mark at his apartment, and then after a period of time, he'd give me a finished track. This went on for a couple of years, and before I knew it, I had enough tracks to release a CD of my stories backed beautifully by Mark and other friends. I started to investigate the possibility of independently releasing a CD. Then my father surprised me and gave me the money to have a thousand CDs burned. It came out really good, I thought. It sold respectably and allowed me to do shows further from home. I've read in Berlin, a few places in Ireland, and around the U.S.A.

I still have yet to contact any publishers about getting my work published in book form. I hope to someday feel confident enough to submit my writing to publishers and see if I can get seen by a wider audience.

In the meantime, I still hustle my way through life. I get occasional work at friends' bars when there is a need for someone to check IDs. I have just released another CD, called *Cut the Gab*, which will help me survive for a few more years. I also collect musical instruments and amplifiers and sell them as the price for these vintage items appreciates. They just don't make them like that anymore. It's not easy work, and things can get tight, but I'm happy and have time to work on what makes me happy: writing!

# Billy Collins

Billy Collins has published ten collections of poetry, the latest being *The Rain in Portugal* (Random House, 2016). He served as United States Poet Laureate (2001-2003) and was recently inducted into the American Academy of Arts and Letters. He is currently a Distinguished Fellow at the Winter Park Institute of Rollins College..

# Bashō in Ireland

I am like the Japanese poet
who longed to be in Kyoto
even though he was already in Kyoto.

I am not exactly like him
because I am not Japanese
and I have no idea what Kyoto is like.

But once while walking around
the Irish town of Ballyvaughan
I caught myself longing to be in Ballyvaughan.

The sensation of being homesick
for a place that is not my home
while being right in the middle of it

was particularly strong
when I passed the hotel bar
then the fluorescent hallway of a washateria,

also when I stood at the crossroads
with the road signs pointing in 3 directions
and the enormous buses making the turn.

It might have had something to do
with the nearby limestone hills
and the rain collecting on my collar,

but then again I have longed
to be with a number of people
while the two of us were sitting in the same room

on an ordinary evening
without a limestone hill in sight,
somewhere thousands of miles from Kyoto

and the simple wonders of Ballyvaughan,
which reminds me
of another Japanese poet

who wrote how much he enjoyed
not being able to see
his favorite mountain because of all the fog.

# Honor Molloy

Honor Molloy is originally from Dublin. Her play *Crackskull Row* yielded a fellowship year at the Radcliffe Institute for Advanced Study at Harvard. Her neo-melodrama, *Madame Killer,* received an NEA Playwriting Fellowship and a Pew Fellowship. Her play *Maiden Voyages* is currently in production. She is also the author of the autobiographical novel *Smarty Girl—Dublin Savage* (2012).

# Writhing in America

When I was eight, I climbed aboard an Aer Lingus aeroplane and took off for the States with my mother and sisters and brothers. Uncle Walter collected us at Kennedy Airport and we stashed our belongings in the boot of a tan station wagon with faux wooden paneling. Why the pretendy wood? In the passenger seat, Mam cuddled weeshy Noelle on her lap. Squashed together in the back were five more Molloys. We'd left one Molloy behind—our da. Was an actor on the telly. Had to emigrate, Mammy said, 'cause he was sick. Drinking, drinking all the time, raging at us all the time, bashing our mam all the time.

Night was rising, Uncle Walter doled out Cool Whip bowls. "There are puke buckets here for the children," he said, afraid one of us would have a spilly-up 'cause we were driving straight through to Pennsylvania, where Mammy grew to tall. As we idled at a stoplight, a taxicab drew up alongside. The taxi man was a chunky Italian, elbow propped casually in the open window. Sweat tickling his neck, one hand on the wheel. I propped my arm on the car door same as him. Casual-like. It was Labor Day weekend, 1969. And I'd come to America for the rest of my life.

We unloaded at midnight, Uncle Walter collected the puke buckets. No one had boaked. We scrambled out of the station wagon like crabs, scuttering up the steps to a cramped flat, the shite end of town. There was a toilet, a kitchen, and two rooms. One for the childer lined with twin mattresses on the floor, no sheets. The second room had a cot for Noelle and a queen-sized mattress for Mammy and my big sister Shivaun to share.

Revving on Irish time, we woke at five the next morning. On the kitchen table, there was a bright yellow box of something called Cheerios. Tasted like plaster. More Cool Whip bowls for to eat our brekkie. Uncle Walter musta loved Cool Whip. Inside a gigantic fridge was an orange block of Land O'Lakes American cheese, already sliced. There was a gallon jug of watery blue milk. Low-fat. So Mammy sent us off in search of bread, rashers, eggs, and real milk.

My older brother Simon clutched a five-dollar bill as we invaded the seedy neighborhood. We'd landed on another planet: streets wide and rubbish bins crowding the pavements. The Allentown Jail loomed over squat row houses tucked in for the night. No sign that a soul was abroad but for light spilling from Rafferty's Grocery at the bottom of our road.

In we went. Rafferty behind the counter, tummy bulging under his apron, jaw on the ground. Sure, it looked like we'd walked out of the past. Simon in gansey and short trousers. Me in the tweed pinafore. Pair of us with scabby knees, loose socks, and round-toed sandals.

"I'd like milk, eggs, bread. And gimme some rashers." "You kids from Ireland?" He was an easy-smiling man, with a ginger crew cut and sticky-out ears.

"How'd you know?"

"My grandmother was from Ballylicky." Rafferty led us about the place loading our arms with groceries. "County Cork. Came over in 1903. We've been here forever."

Wonder. Wonder what this is? Bread? Marshmallow, more like. Polka dots on the bag? Go way. Bought it anyway 'cause it seemed like a toy.

"What about the rashers?"

"Rashers?""Rashers. Meat. From a pig. Comes in strips.""All right, ahhm—how 'bout this?"I lifted a red-and-yellow package from the refrigerated case. Oscar Mayer. Flipped it over. There was a see-through window in the back. White fat with a teeny stripe of red. S'not rashers. Rashers came in raw slabs, piled on brown paper. Whole pigs swung in Magill's window. Blood spilt on the sawdusty floor. Cow's eyes up for sale. Bunnies and lambs, yours for the taking. Grim butcher, white smock smeared in animal blood.

"Or this?" Rafferty plunked down a plastic packet. Inside: a circular stack of pinky meat. Oscar Mayer again. Who's this Oscar Mayer when he's home?

Back at the flat, "Baloney?" Mammy says. "You brought me baloney. Where are the rashers?"

I eyed Simon. Simon eyed me. The food at Rafferty's was wrapped and boxed, hidden away. We couldn't tell from rashers.

"I detest baloney," Mam wailed, wrecked from our journey cross the sea. "I asked you for rashers."

"They didn't have any."

"Course they have bacon." Mam's American accent was stronger since she'd come home. "Every shop has bacon."

"What's bacon?"

"Rashers," Mam cried.

Rafferty's daughter, Toodie, was in third grade. Like me. She ordered me to throw out my Bradley's sandals 'cause they were square. *Square.* A new word. Meant old-fashioned. Toodie gave me a pair of lime-green plastic shoes with a hint of a heel. Mammy hated them shoes 'cause they smacked of teenhood. I clattered round the apartment in them green plastic shoes, dancing in a butterscotch frock from my American Gran. Brand new, only for me. When I pulled that frock down over my head, I pulled on an American self.

One September day, after school, Toodie and I sat on her bed playing with dolls from around the world: the Dutch girl with plaits and wooden shoes; the Spanish niña in her Flamenco rig-out; and the Irish colleen. The Irish colleen had roaring red hairs down to her bum, eight freckles on her face—four on each cheek—and a hunter-green plaid dress, gold buckle at the waist, white lace at the hem. Toodie was a redhead, too. She had so many-many freckles it looked like diseases.

"I have red hair. Like this doll. I have freckles. Like this doll," Toodie boasted. "So I'm more Irish than you."

How dare she? I was born there. What a terrible fake of a girl. Only put up with me 'cause her daddy forced her. Lucky she had a daddy. So I punched her in the eye. Walked on from her house, no lookbacks.

Throughout my early days in this country, I had a recurring dream: I'm bolting over O'Connell Bridge. The Liffey flowing beneath. My father's chasing me. I glance back to gauge how close when I see the gun. And Da shoots me in the back. Heat. Grows and it grows, the heat. Spreads through me. Am I dead? Did he kill me? It's then I find myself on Hamilton Street, Allentown's main thoroughfare. Not Dublin at all.

My final Patrick's Day in Ireland I got caught in a peace demonstration bound for the North. The Molloy kids marched all the way to Bray, singing "We Shall Overcome." A year later, there I was, crushed in the Paddy's Day hordes—diddle-dee-die-doh, kill-me music patootling from passing floats. Utterly disgusted by Allentown's version of What's Irish: the green hair, the pots o' gold. What shambolicals.

I wanted no part of this portrayal of my country. So within six months of our landing, I lost the accent, dumped the tweed, and drowned myself in Yankee slang.

NYC—Monthly Rents, 1981–2004
Lower East Side, 1981: $160
East Village, 1982: $250
TriBeCa, 1985: $200
Upper East Side, 1987: $360
Brooklyn, 1992: $200

TriBeCa, 1994–2004: $600

Acting brought me to New York. It was the eighties. Time was plentiful and rent was cheap. Bargain real estate provided the opportunity to study and make theater in the world's most vibrant city.

I was reading playscripts, writing grants, and building a new theater company with friends. About that time, Willy Holtzman cast me in *The Last Temptation of Joe Hill*, his one-act that touched upon the Granite Mountain Mine disaster of 1917. I played an Irish woman who'd lost her husband in the devastating fire that took the lives of 168 miners. As I prepared for the role, I practiced the accent I'd abandoned years before. Reshaping vowels, final consonants, shattering a two-syllable word into three, maybe four. Ireland sprang alive in my mouth, the smells and the swells of Dublin.

I auditioned for Wynn Handman's acting class with Willy's monologue and got accepted. When Wynn suggested Molly Bloom's soliloquy, I was, as my Auntie Marguerite said, away in a hack. Famous for developing and directing solo shows with Eric Bogosian and John Leguizamo, Wynn encouraged me to write and act my own material. Acting Irish led me to writing Irish.

I brought bibs and bobs to class and tried them out in gritty downtown venues. This material became Molloy—a performance piece about my father's and grandfather's addiction to alcohol, violence, and the theater. The Irish Arts Center hosted the first evening-long presentation. When I ran into producer Nye Heron years later, he said, "Jaysus, I saw that. There are still pieces of your father spattered on the back walls of this theater." With rock-bottom rent, the occasional lend of subway tokens from my pals, living on seltzer and popcorn, I could afford to tear around the East Village at three in the morning with a wheat-paste bucket, slapping up posters for pieces about:

the Birmingham Church Bombing of '63; Senators Helms and D'Amato's attack on the NEA; Lesbian Cheek. And don't forget Rehearsin' the Granda; Me, the Howlin'; and Murphy—all variations on Molloy. Seems there was no getting away from the dada.

I met the mighty Bronagh Murphy—nurse, midwife, and actor—in 1988. We spent five years developing *Maiden Voyages,* a play set in the Rotunda, Dublin's oldest maternity hospital. Word that we were auditioning spread like wildfire. Dozens of Irish women showed up, "Missus. Come here to me. Don't have a résumé. And I certainly don't have a pic."

This was my first play. It wasn't political sketch comedy, a monologue, or a dance-theater work. Bronagh and I blended contemporary and ancient women's stories with rich humor and Dublin's salty vernacular. One night at Sin-é bar, we heard Susan McKeown and the Chanting House. So we cast Susan as the ghost of the Roto, who sings from behind the walls.

I got married. Got a job. Wrote plays. I'd research and gather and think. Earwig and research some more. Every few years I'd take a vacation and write a first draft flat-out in nine days. I wrote plays. Had a job. Was married. In my marriage was told I was nothing, that my writing was nothing. Had a job. Was married. Was nothing. Became my mother, trapped in the past with my da. Married-was-married. Was nothing. Two sisters in marriages like mine. Wrote plays about slips of mind, slips of time, slips of rage. Of incest and murder and Ireland.

And the plays stayed in the drawer. Never saw production.

Upon a time in TriBeCa, I walked out of that ten-year marriage and left a self behind. Moved to Brooklyn and spent ages composing *Smarty Girl—Dublin Savage,* a novel about my childhood. One chapter took a year. Forty pages. One year. So much time in the sad mess of the back-there, hunting my father in the dark, desperate to understand him and the dire effect he had on our family. How did he become such a broken man?

Could I ever forgive him? And after decades and decades, finding suddenly that I did. Forgive him. And love him, too.

As I approached publication, I presented readings from *Smarty Girl* for New York's Irish and Irish-American communities. At first I was full of apprehension about how I'd be received, afraid my writing would be dismissed. Perhaps my version of Ireland wasn't accurate because it was based on distant recollections. I'd had to construct a great deal. I mean, how much of my past is fiction? And? Was there a Toodie Rafferty in the crowd claiming to be more Irish than me?

I joined the Irish American Writers and Artists—a gang that held monthly salons at the Upper West Side's Bar Thalia. On any given night, there'd be ten-twelve punters keening, crooning, acting, drooling, picking, strumming, and reading. We shared poems and stories and songs about daddies and mams and grannies and cousins and gangsters and brudders and nuns. We made each other laugh and cry, often at the same time, in sudden recognition. "That's my family. We did that too."

Many times a presenter choked up with an overwhelming feeling that threatened to bring her down. But the audience was there, do you know. And we made it through together—stronger from the effort.

Through writing you can find a way to yourself. A way to quench the anger and the sadness. To mend the split between that land and this. That land of trepidation and penury. This land of confidence and dreams.

When did America become home? When I moved to New York. When I joined the New York Irish Communities. These days, I go easy among the Irish. Because my home is not a nation, it's being a writer. These days, I say, "Don't look back. Don't look down. Look to up. Leap. Keep. In the leap."

# John F. Kennedy Jr.

*(November 25, 1960 – July 16, 1999)*

Born into the White House, the only son to the most beloved president in U.S. history and a mother who was one of the most influential fashion figures of the twentieth century, John F. Kennedy Jr. seemed preordained to soar.

On his third birthday, he was the focus of one of the most iconic photographs ever taken when he was snapped saluting his father's casket outside Saint Matthew's Cathedral in Washington, D.C. For the next thirty-five years of his life, the camera lens would continue to hound his every move. The media portrayed him as the sole heir to Camelot. He was a modern-day Irish-American prince. By the time he was twenty-eight, *People* magazine had landed him on its cover, branding him Sexiest Man Alive. It was a superficial title he was keen to transcend.

Throughout his years at Brown University, Kennedy had been interested in theater, so it was no surprise that after he graduated, he decided to give acting a shot. In 1985, he made his Manhattan debut in a Brian Friel play on the stage of the Irish

Arts Center. Artistic director Nye Heron claimed Kennedy was "one of the best young actors I've seen in years." But neither the time nor the circumstances were quite right for Kennedy's acting career. It would be the last time he would ever perform on stage.

In July 1990, he passed the New York Bar exam and went to work for the Manhattan District Attorney's Office for four years. But his heart was not in it. It was his love of writing, journalism in particular, that really fueled his imagination.

In 1992, he published his first piece in *The New York Times*. The writing in that early work is strong, clear, and fluid, with hints of Hemingway or Theroux. But again, the notion of embracing the life of a writer full-heartedly and facing the harsh gaze of the critics must have been a terrifying prospect. John F. Kennedy was too self-aware to believe that he would ever be judged by the same barometer as other mere mortals; he was a Kennedy first and foremost, and the press was never going to forgive him for that.

But if Kennedy couldn't write, perhaps he could influence conversation through editing. With its tagline of "Not Just Politics as Usual," the first issue of Kennedy's *George* magazine premiered in October 1995 with Cindy Crawford gracing the cover posed as George Washington. It was one of the biggest magazine launches in history, with an initial print run of two million copies. It was an enormous gamble.

The magazine was met instantly with criticism for Kennedy's attempt to marry celebrity culture and politics. In retrospect, it would seem, he was way ahead of his time.

The publication of the magazine also landed him back in the public eye, and for the next few years, as he tried to establish the magazine as a place for respected journalism, members of the press hunted him relentlessly on the streets of his beloved New York City. In the end, they were practically camped outside the

TriBeCa loft he shared with his new bride, Carolyn Bessette-Kennedy. He was born in a gilded cage, and they were going to make sure he stayed there, like some mutant circus freak.

For the next few years, it seemed you couldn't pick up a New York daily newspaper without seeing a picture of Kennedy cycling or rollerblading to and from work at the office of *George* magazine. In pictures from the time, he appears driven, introspective…a man on a mission. He was also driven to fly, ignoring pleas from friends and his mother's premonitions that it would prove fatal.

Rarely has a celebrity in New York suffered such brutal scrutiny. Sadly, he was never to know what it felt like to be free of that burden.

On July 16, 1999, the Piper Saratoga John F. Kennedy Jr. was piloting on his way to a wedding on Martha's Vineyard crashed into the Atlantic Ocean, killing Kennedy, his wife, Carolyn, and her sister Lauren. He was only thirty-eight years old.

Colin Broderick

# Colum McCann

Colum McCann was born in Dublin in 1965 and began his career as a journalist at *The Irish Press*. In the early 1980s he took a bicycle across North America and then worked as a wilderness guide in a program for juvenile delinquents in Texas. After a year and a half in Japan, he and his wife, Allison, moved to New York, where they currently live with their three children, Isabella, John Michael, and Christian. McCann's fiction has been published in over 40 languages. He won the National Book Award with his 2009 novel, *Let the Great World Spin*. His short film *Everything in This Country Must* was nominated for an Academy Award in 2005. McCann teaches in the creative writing program at Hunter College in New York and is the co-founder of the global non-profit Narrative 4.

# The New York Book of the Dead

In the mid-1980s I lived in rural Texas. I was a wilderness counselor in a camp for juvenile delinquents. Six teenagers and I lived in pine-pole shelters in an out-of-the-way creekbed. The purpose was to give them time to confront their lives, their problems, their demons. They would emerge after three months and then move to an on-campus school. The days were stacked with things to do. We built an outdoor latrine and gravity-fed showers. We grew a small garden. We occasionally took trips, rock-climbing and kayaking. We slept out every night. The stars were like bullet holes above us. The mornings broke hard and hot. We worked all day, exhausted ourselves. I became an inhabitant of what it meant to be on the edge of wild. The boys had all been through tough lives. Most of them had spent time in juvenile detention. In their family lives they had seen despair. But at night I would read them to sleep. *The Grapes of Wrath*. *Catcher in the Rye*. A fable called "Fup," by Jim Dodge. They had never been read to before, but amazingly they fell asleep to the stories. I was already consumed by literature, and I was moved by the power it had over these kids, who had seen more despair and violence than my imagination might ever offer.

I was in my early twenties and wanted to be a writer. Much as I liked the wilderness camp, I was sure that I had to get away. I would lie back on my pine-pole bed and dream of going to New York. I'd wear a dark overcoat and a black beret and affect for myself a Kerouac way of walking.

The dream of most of us is the dream of being elsewhere. New York seemed to hold elsewhere like no other place. I had already spent a few months there when I was eighteen years old, fresh from Ireland, but I wanted to return. To slip into the pattern of the writing life. Enough of all these gravity-fed showers. No more tree branches. No more cricketsong. I needed to get away from Texas.

At night, in the camp, after the boys were asleep, I would slip away from the creekbed to go smoke a cigarette, which was, I suppose, as close to literary cliché as I could get. The boys, of course, were not allowed to smoke, and I didn't want to set a bad example. So I drifted along the creekbed, over a few fences. and lay in a nearby grass field, blowing smoke rings at the dark and dreaming my writerly life, wandering through the Village on the arms of beautiful women, bringing a brigade of drunks to the White Horse Tavern, reading aloud at the Bowery Club.

Later I strolled back through the kleingrass towards the camp, where I checked the tree houses to make sure all the boys were asleep. (Occasionally they would run away, but they inevitably returned because they were "afraid of the dark.") I hid my cigarettes and drifted off to sleep. My imagination turned the corner onto St. Mark's Place. I joined the little riot of language down there by Tompkins Square Park, turned towards the Bowery once more.

I lived in New York for a summer when I was a teenager. At that age, naivete can overcome reality—when I first came to the city, I didn't even mind the cockroaches that littered the floor of the tiny room I rented in Brighton Beach for $120 a month. I worked in Manhattan, a runner for a press syndicate, dropping off envelopes and getting sandwiches for the bosses. I came home every night on the D train, heroic with beer and cocaine and youth. I was either too stupid or too broke to get mugged. I recall standing transfixed in the middle of the pavement one night, people stepping blithely around me as I stared up at the Time-Life building, watching the lights flicker on and off in the upper floors, thinking if there was nothing else in my life, there would always, at least, be this. A gorgeous rubbish heap of a city.

Eventually I worked my way through the ranks and began reporting, but after a few months I returned to Ireland again.

I still had the Broadway glare in my eyes, but it was almost eight years, the early nineties, before I got a chance to live in New York again.

I left the wilderness camp, got myself a degree in Austin, Texas, married, roamed, went to Japan, returned to Ireland for a while, published a book of short stories, scratched out a novel, *Songdogs*, then found myself with a chance to properly live in the city that supposedly never slept.

It wasn't quite what it had seemed when it was dreamed: It was more a city of ceilings. I was a young husband. I wore an open-neck shirt. We found an apartment in the rather pedestrian Murray Hill. I had to make the rent. I taught English as a Second Language in a midtown school. It all seemed rather mannered. I felt hemmed in by the city. Dust on the windowsill. I began to think that I had made a grave mistake.

Still, there was always the possibility of escape. I took long walks. I abandoned myself for hours, searching for a sight of myself on the other side of the street. I hung around a little in Sin-é, down on Eighth Street, where the cool young Irish emigrants hung out, but I didn't necessarily want to be Irish, I wanted to be something else, away from all that, rid of history. That elusive elsewhere hung over me. That otherness. That shadow-shadow. I wanted to fit into my prefabricated idea of the city, but I just couldn't find it. Surely I could be someone other than this housebroken young writer I had become?

I was working as an ESL teacher. The city seemed more interested in money than language, or perhaps it was because I had to pay almost $1,000 a month in rent. I began to miss the days that I had spent out in the wilderness of Texas. There had been a freedom there. This was a city that was going to paralyze me.

One summer afternoon I made my way to Chumley's, the downtown bar on Bedford, a former speakeasy, famous among generations of writers. Steinbeck had been a customer. So too had Dos Passos, Eugene O'Neill, William Faulkner. I wanted to soak in the atmosphere. I sat down and began scribbling bitter nothings in a notebook. I had only enough money for one beer and the bar was more or less deserted. I nursed my clichés. Even they exhausted themselves. The beer glass was empty. The afternoon darkened. When I got outside, the rain was skittering down. It was a three- or four-mile walk home. No money even for the subway. I was at my lowest point. So I walked. In the thunderstorm. Sirens. Shoulders. Puddle splash. Fuck this town. Its gravity, its pressure, its filth. Fuck it. I was soaked. I would leave. Pack up and go. Fuck it.

I took off my shirt, wrapped it around my head, and started walking quickly through the crowds. Soaked to the skin, angry, pissed off, confused. Through the Village, up near the Flatiron. Still the rain hammered down. But the walking eased me a little, took the pressure off. This was not how it was meant to be. A novelist without a city. In the city to which all novelists seemed to aspire. I began to talk to myself. Nobody seemed to notice. I talked louder, continuing on up near the New York Public Library. Straight up Fifth Avenue towards the park. At this stage, I was almost shouting. I barreled on. And then a strange sense of calm and relief washed over me. This is a wilderness. Nobody cares. You can do whatever you want. It was very simple. I had spent all my time caring about the city, and the simple fact of the matter was that the city did not give a good goddamn about me. I was, in essence, back in the Texas camp. I could be there. And anywhere. A new elsewhere. Such great liberation. Such a joy. I could spend some time in an open-neck shirt. All that mattered was the work. That was enough. In fact, that was all.

I went home to write.

I love this town. I love that I can even call it a town. Eight million or ten million or two million, it doesn't matter, this is a symphony of a place. That's part of what makes it great for a writer. It assaults the senses at every angle. One realizes that there are stories everywhere. There is an attitude in the city, a sort of swaggering that occurs in the head and the heart and the mouth. I don't know of any other city in the world where you go and immediately feel as if you belong—and yet still also be true to your home country. I am a New Yorker and an Irishman and I see absolutely no contradiction in this. In fact, most of the city is an immigrant culture. You can walk through the borough of Queens on any given day and hear two dozen different languages being spoken on the same street—a true Babel.

And so it is a city not so much of America as of the world: a mirror to the pure anarchy of the human condition.

They say you know where you're from when you know where you want to die. First off, I'd be happy to be scattered, as most of my life has been. And while part of me would like to be thrown to the wind in Dublin, where I was born, or the West of Ireland, where I escaped for a while, or the North of Ireland, which is a heart-home of mine, or even Texas, or France, or Italy, I think I'd like most of me to be thrown into the wind over Manhattan to end up wherever the breeze happens to take me—the corner of a room in the Chelsea, the dark of a Second Avenue bar, in the dust of the paths of Central Park, in the spin of a Coney Island dodgem car, in the grime that settles on the fire escapes of the Lower East Side.

New York. Living here makes it a good place even when you're dead.

"You walk through a series of arches, so to speak, and then, presently, at the end of a corridor, a door opens and you see backward through time, and you feel the flow of time, and realize you are only part of a great nameless procession."

## *John Huston*
*(August 5, 1906–August 28, 1987)*

# John Kearns

John Kearns is the author of the short-story collection *Dreams and Dull Realities* and the novel *The World*. His novel-in-progress, *Worlds*, was a finalist in the 2002 New Century Writers' Awards. He has had five full-length and five one-act plays produced in Manhattan, including *In the Wilderness*, *Sons of Molly Maguire*, and *In a Bucket of Blood*. His fiction has appeared in *The Medulla Review* and *Danse Macabre*. Kearns has a Master's Degree in Irish Literature from the Catholic University of America. He is the producer of a weekly literary salon in Manhattan, which he runs in association with Irish American Writers and Artists.

# Bronx Thunder to Riverside Angels

I scrawled my first words as a New York City writer by candlelight during a thunderstorm in Little Italy of the Bronx. The tiny apartment in the eighty-two-year-old tenement had a hole in its ceiling and, as yet, no electricity. I had just turned twenty-two and earned a B.A. in English from Saint Joseph's University.

When I had told people that after graduation I would be leaving comfortable suburban Philadelphia for the Bronx, they said I might as well move to a war zone. Nobody understood. It didn't make sense—except in the basic way that I was a writer and that writers go to New York. And my friend from Saint Joe's Prep had just graduated from Fordham and knew the neighborhood.

In Philadelphia, I had published stories and poems in the literary magazines of Saint Joe's Prep and University, composed a hefty manuscript of a novel titled *11* during an honors independent-study course, assembled my poems and songs into a thirty-minute show performed at university coffee houses and Cavanaugh's Bothy Club, and filled numerous journals. But ever since that candlelit thunderstorm in Belmont—with the exception of sojourns in West Philadelphia, Vermont, and Washington, D.C.,—I have been a New York City writer.

During my early days in the Bronx, I was young enough to pass for a college student. So using an entrance near Belmont Avenue where there was no security guard, I would sneak onto Fordham's campus and work in a study-hall room.

My short story "Flight" served as a literary bridge between Philadelphia, where it was started on May 21, 1986, and the Bronx, where the draft was completed on June 11. Six years later, "Flight" would be my first short story to be published professionally. Once I wrote a whole short story about a teenaged South Bronx girl, "It's All Abandoned," in one study-hall sitting. Both stories appear in my collection *Dreams and Dull Realities*.

So from the start, my New York City writing has been a guerrilla activity in which, fighting the interruptions and distractions of city life, I seek out and occupy spaces where I can concentrate, such as:

The McDonald's across from the Empire State Building on my first day exploring Manhattan, the benches in Central Park during every ad-agency lunch hour, a Wall Street atrium…As a teacher at Saint Pius V High School in the South Bronx, I had less leisure time, and so I had to set up a routine for myself. When the Bronx 55 bus would deposit me in front of Saint Barnabas Hospital on Third Avenue, I would walk up Arthur Avenue past Emilia's, Dominick's, Randazzo's Fish Market, and Addeo Bakery to the Enrico Fermi Library at 186th and Hughes. I would force myself to stay there as long as I could stand it. Often the atmosphere was far from bookish. Elementary school kids would be hanging out pretending to do homework. Sometimes high school kids would be there, too—including girls from Aquinas wearing the same gray skirts and blue tunics as the Saint Pius girls—and their chatter and gum cracking would prove intolerable. I have often wondered how much the lengths of the sections in my story "Dreams and Dull Realities" were influenced by the length of time I was able to remain in the Fermi Library.

…Father Demo Park, Telegraphe Cafe, Duke's Cafe in Times Square, a bench by Sixth and Bleecker, the New York Public Library's Rose Reading Room, the Mid-Manhattan Library…

Periods of unemployment have always been great boons to my creative output.

In 1990 in West Philadelphia, in between teaching religion

and proofreading ads, I wrote and typed my first full-length play, *In the Wilderness,* about a South Bronx high school. Smoking cigarettes and downing pots of tea, I heard the clatter and chimes of the New York subway in the clacking and ringing of my typewriter. I kept reworking the play over the years, and it came to life in 2012.

When I was unemployed and writing my novel *The World* in 1992, I used to spread my papers and notebooks on a table in the Mid-Manhattan Library. There were plenty of homeless people and shifty-looking characters around, and each table bore signs warning readers that the library was not responsible for lost or stolen items. So I couldn't move from my chair—even to go to the bathroom—without taking everything with me. This produced a lot of manuscript pages.

During lean times in 2001 and 2002, I spent many afternoons with a laptop and the manuscript of my novel in progress, *Worlds,* in the Science, Industry and Business Library. After writing plays for a decade, I returned to this novel and will complete it in 2015.

…Bosie Tea Parlor, the public plaza by Rockefeller Center, Cafe Europa by the Ed Sullivan Theater, the Columbia Teachers College Lounge, the Staten Island Ferry…

When I lived in Saint George, Staten Island, and proofread for an advertising agency, I had no student papers to grade and was able to write on the ferry and during lunch. Still, this didn't seem like enough. So one morning, before heading down to the boat, I got up early and took a seat at the kitchen table. I completed about a sentence when I was startled by movement on the other side of the kitchen. I spied a large mouse leaping out from behind one counter and in a single bound concealing itself behind the other. That marked the first and last day of this writing routine.

My longest-lasting writing routine, in place for nearly a

decade, occurs after work hours, when I stay in or near my office. Sometimes I edit drafts on the office computer or on a laptop in a cafe or park. Other times I print pages and edit them on a bench or in a deli and input the changes the next day. Starting with light editing helps with the transition from technical to creative writing. I start by fixing typos or commas and soon find myself fully immersed in writing and rewriting.

When I get ideas away from a computer, I jot them in a pocket notebook. Ideas stop me in my tracks on the street and even on subway platforms with passengers rushing around me. Now that I have a smartphone, I email ideas to myself and copy them to my current manuscript.

Over the years, I have lived like an artist under cover, working through the day as a responsible employee while keeping my true identity a secret. Most people struggle to keep their professional and personal lives separate. However, for me it is more than just protecting my personal life; it is hiding what I consider my true vocation. At every job, I wonder whether to expose my writing life and how much. At times, I have been encouraged to speak about it and invite coworkers to plays and readings, only to suffer for it later. At other times, I have received remarkable support from coworkers and managers. The tension between work and art requires delicate handling.

In addition to teaching in the South Bronx and proofreading ads, I have had to support myself in a number of odd ways:

Telephone interviewer of farmers, web-design salesman to restaurants, reader for a blind man in D.C., salesman of *El Diario de Mexico* to bodegas in Queens and Spanish Harlem...

But the main work I have done for nearly twenty years is technical writing, a career I stumbled upon by accident. At a freelance writing job in D.C., a lawyer referred to me as a technical writer and I looked up the term at the Library of

Congress. I discovered pages of citations, many published by the Society for Technical Communication (STC). (Years later I would become vice president and then president of the New York Metro Chapter of the STC.)

As a technical writer, I write for a living without prostituting my talent. I master subject matter from experts and communicate it in a clear, concise way to people who need it. Establishing my technical writing career was a struggle, however. I had to take a course at the USDA Graduate School and move from Maryland to Vermont for my first full-time job at IBM. With a year's experience, I was able to return to New York, after five long years away, as an employee of Popkin Software. Since then I have worked for a series of software companies and larger corporations like Morgan Stanley and NBCUniversal.

Technical writing has given me fodder for creative writing as well: I have had a front-row seat for the information revolution, the e-commerce bubble, the 2008 financial crisis, and now, at NBCUniversal, for the transformation of how television programming is consumed. Plus, in addition to keeping body and soul together, technical writing has helped fund play productions, publications, and trips to give readings and lectures.

At the end of my second school year at Saint Pius V, I turned my sweltering 187th Street apartment into a story-submissions factory, a somewhat involved task back in the days of typewriters and self-addressed stamped envelopes (SASEs). Referring to the fat hardback *Writer's Market*, I mailed short stories to literary magazines. Over the next few months, I came home to the disappointment of SASEs stuffed in the cramped mailbox.

In Philadelphia in 1990, I sent out copies of *In the Wilderness* in larger envelopes, with the same results. When I worked in advertising, I had access to a computer and printer for the first time and was able to make more submissions. There were many walks to midtown mailboxes during which I counted off decades of the rosary on my fingers. But I kept receiving those envelopes bearing my handwriting.

In August 1992, I moved to the Washington, D.C., area to earn my M.A. in English with an Irish Literature Concentration from the Catholic University of America. I had studied so much about Irish literature, history, and culture that it made sense to make things official with a diploma. Once school started, there would be little time for creative writing, let alone submitting stories. So it seemed all my mailings had been for naught.

However, shortly after the move, I got a call from my dad saying he'd received forwarded mail from Connecticut. The letter said my short story "Flight" had won second prize in a fiction contest, had been read aloud at a festival, published, and awarded twenty-five dollars. It was my first publication! I put the twenty-five dollars in a drawer and never spent it.

Today I refer to *Poets & Writers* magazine for submission and contest deadlines, and I maintain a Word document tracking story, poem, and play submissions. I mark rejections in gray shaded dates and acceptances in green bold digits. There are many more boxes with gray shading than there are with triumphant green characters, but I have been fortunate to have my work published in prestigious literary magazines like *The North American Review* and *Grey Sparrow Journal*, and to have an excerpt from my novel-in-progress, *Worlds*, named a finalist in the 2002 New Century Writers' Award.

A tremendous benefit to the New York writer, however, is the ample opportunity to give readings and to have plays produced—and I frequently pass these old venues in my travels:

The Eugene Frankel Theatre, Rocky Sullivan's, the 11th Street Bar, the Bowery Poetry Club...In 1998, I was working at Popkin Software when I got a voice mail message from Colum McCann asking me to read at the Young Irish Writers evening at the American Irish Historical Society (AIHS). This thrilling evening marks the beginning of the public presentation of my writing.

Since that time, I have done numerous readings and had five full-length and five one-act plays on New York stages. My first produced one-act was directed by a coworker who had heard about my reading at the AIHS. My other one-act plays have been in festivals around Manhattan: "Hanging Questions" was an 8-Minute-Madness finalist and "I Knew You'd Say That!" made the finals of the Strawberry One-Act Festival. My first staged full-length play, the Irish-gangster comedy *Designers with Dirty Faces,* had a debut reading at the suitably Cagney-esque Rocky Sullivan's. Its first full production occurred at the Crosby-esque Little Theatre of Saint Mary's in Woodside. I directed, ran the sound, and even acted in one scene. The play broke box-office records, and attendees said they had more fun than at far costlier shows on Broadway.

…the Robert Moss Theatre, the Morningside Book Shop, 2A, the Bleecker Street Theatre, Marty O'Brien's…After *Designers with Dirty Faces* played in Manhattan in the Fashion PlayFest, one of the actors suggested I write a serious play about Hell's Kitchen gangsters. The result was *In a Bucket of Blood,* which became the founding show of Plays Upstairs at Ryan's Daughter pub and was a success in the Midtown International Theatre Festival (MITF). I developed the theme of Irish organized crime further with *Sons of Molly Maguire,* which played on MITF's main stage. My other full-length plays, *Resignations* and *In the Wilderness,* about office workers and a South Bronx high school, ran in the Planet Connections Theatre Festivity.

…Where Eagles Dare Theatre, the Knitting Factory, Ontological-Hysteric Theatre, Turtle's Shell Theatre, TSI/PlayTime…

In 2002, an agent showed interest in my novel *The World* but wanted to sell my collection of short stories first. She read a couple of stories and asked for the rest. I began jokingly beginning sentences with, "My agent..." Then one out-of-work day I came home to find the entire collection returned. The agent wrote that the stories were "terrific" but "without a track record" the collection would be difficult to sell. This was a crushing disappointment.

Soon I got a new job, got back on my feet, and got involved in theater. Impatient with the mainstream process, I self-published my novel through iUniverse. I was able to sell copies at play performances and readings, but it proved hard to get it on bookstore shelves. I published *Dreams and Dull Realities* though a small press, Boann Books and Media LLC, and did a lousy job of marketing it because of another layoff and the start of a new job.

Happily, I still get stories and poems published from time to time, and I will be pursuing an agent for my novel *Worlds* this year.


I have been passionate about my Irish heritage from the day I was told not to be.

Since moving to New York, I have followed Irish culture. I was probably the only person buying *The Irish Echo* on Little Italy's 187th Street every week. I devoured Irish literature and history, books I had not gotten to in school. Ulick O'Connor's *All the Olympians* about the Irish Literary Renaissance is one I recall, and I loved Richard Ellman's biography of James Joyce. I listened to WFUV's Irish shows. Up on Bainbridge Avenue, there were film screenings and lectures about the Troubles. I enjoyed traditional music concerts at the Eagle Tavern and the trad festival in Snug Harbor, Staten Island.

I attended Irish readings and plays. Not knowing it was any big deal, I caught the Irish Repertory Theatre's first production, *Juno and the Paycock*. I took my beaten copy of *Ulysses* to

"Bloomsday on Broadway" every year from 1987.

I never missed a Saint Patrick's Day Parade on Fifth Avenue, even in the bitter cold or the rain. When I was in graduate school, I was appalled that my presentation on Yeats's *The Tower* was scheduled for March 17th. It meant spending a Saint Patrick's Day in Washington, D.C., which I wouldn't wish on a drunken vainglorious lout.

From attending so many Irish events, I began to recognize and meet many writers and musicians, but I was very much on the periphery. Growing up in Philadelphia, I had never been involved in Irish organizations.

However, for the past five years, I have been part of Irish American Writers and Artists (IAW&A), have worked with incredible talents, and made good friends. Through the IAW&A, artists who might have been isolated in tenement apartments or libraries, as I was, encourage and promote one another's work. I am grateful that the board has trusted me to be its treasurer for three years.

I have also been the producer of the IAW&A Salon, evenings in which member artists share ten-minute samples of their work, for two years. In the salon, I have a supportive, attentive Irish-American artistic community and a venue in which to share new writing twice a month. It has led to some marvelous opportunities like taking the salon on the road to Connecticut, Philadelphia, and Washington, D.C., and having an online salon with Dublin writers. I have also given readings and lectures in Ireland and talked about the Molly Maguires on the top radio show in the country. In October 2014, I was honored to host the Eugene O'Neill Lifetime Achievement Award for Pete Hamill, a party crashed by Andrew Cuomo, the governor of New York.

I moved to the Bronx with no graspable reason for doing so. But now, I have myriad concrete reasons to be in New York—including the IAW&A, NBCU, and the life I have built here. Before I moved to Morningside Heights from Yorkville, I had a dream that I was high on a hill writing, surrounded by slender angels playing trumpets. I later learned that these angels resembled statues atop Riverside Church. I have lived in that neighborhood for almost ten years now and have written several plays and my six-hundred-page *Worlds* manuscript.

Here's to more music from the angels.

# Brendan Behan

*(February 9, 1923–March 20, 1964)*

It's nighttime, Greenwich Village, 1962. A hulking figure in a long black coat drunkenly barrels across Broadway in search of a bar. Trying to keep pace by his side is a wiry-haired folk singer just in from Minnesota. The playwright is oblivious to the young man's presence—he has only one thing on his mind:

more booze. The denizens of the White Horse Tavern that night probably paid little heed to the scene playing out in the corner as moments later a twenty-year-old Bob Dylan sat quietly witnessing a bloated thirty-nine-year old Brendan Behan pass out on the table before him.

The life of Brendan Behan is peppered with such legendary anecdotes. No other Irish writer in history gave himself so fully to the artifice of notoriety. It was a life so monumentally tragic that it has almost eclipsed all mention of the work he produced.

Behan was born in Dublin on the 9th of February, 1923, to a pair of fiercely republican parents. By the time he was eight, a neighbor spotted him staggering down the street with his grandmother one afternoon. "Oh, my!" said the neighbor "Isn't it terrible ma'am to see such a beautiful child deformed?" "How dare you," snapped his grandmother. "He's not deformed, he's just drunk!"At the age of sixteen Behan joined the IRA. Within months, he was arrested for possession of explosives on his way to blow up the Liverpool docks. He was sentenced to three years in Borstal. The experience provided him the material for his first autobiography, *Borstal Boy.*

Once released from Borstal, Behan returned to Dublin and remained free, briefly, before being imprisoned again for the attempted murder of two detectives. He was given fourteen years but was released after three on amnesty.

It was in prison that Behan's writing career was born. In Mountjoy Prison, he wrote his first play and some short stories and poetry. His first pieces were published in *The Bell,* a famous Irish literary magazine of the time.

By 1946, he was back in jail again, for trying to free a prisoner from jail in Manchester.

It's possible that Behan grew tired of being locked away for his misdeeds. He was a sloppy criminal. In the early 1950s, after his third release from prison, he went off to Paris, where he made a living for a spell writing pornography. But as reckless as he was, even he could see that it was work not befitting his talent. He began writing more seriously, contributing to some of the best Irish publications of the time, and in 1954 he had a breakthrough with his prison play, *The Quare Fellow.* The work was a huge success in Ireland, then London, and by late 1958 it was on a New York stage.

Behan wrote his next play, *The Hostage,* in Gaelic. In 1958 it was translated into English and in quick succession bounced from Dublin to London to Broadway.

In September 1960, thirty-seven-year-old Brendan Behan arrived on American soil for the first time to the flash and pop of camera bulbs and a sea of extended microphones. The New York press had gotten wind of this wild Irish playwright who had already gained notoriety in London for his drunken antics. Behan was renowned for showing up at his own play, three sheets to the wind, and joining the actors on stage mid-performance, much the amusement of the audience and the critics. But Behan had been warned ahead of time by the Broadway producers of his show, and by his long-suffering wife, Beatrice, who was by his side for the trip, that no such circus would be entertained on a New York stage. And so he arrived in America for the first time clear-eyed and sober, telling the crush of reporters at the airport, "I will drink tea, coffee, and soda while I'm in America." Someone handed him a glass of milk and he held it aloft for the cameras, grinning like an innocent schoolboy. Behan was going to be on his best behavior.

And he was…for a short while.

For the first weeks Brendan Behan was in America, he took New York by storm. The gregarious, witty Irishman was the toast of the town. The press trailed him everywhere. From his home base at the famed Algonquin Hotel, Behan devoured Manhattan from top to bottom. He talked to strangers on the street, held court in random bars, telling jokes, singing Irish rebel songs, handing out money to those who needed it. He loved New York, and New York loved him right back. He was an instantaneous star. Jack Parr, the most famous television talk-show host in America, had Behan guest-host his show one night. Jackie Gleason, arguably the most famous celebrity in America at the time, hunted him down and announced to the world that he and Behan were working together on a series of writing projects. He was invited to parties by the likes of Tennessee Williams and the Marx Brothers. Brendan Behan was an overnight sensation.

Then came the coat.

For the first time in his life, Brendan was flush. He signed a $15,000 book deal. He was being paid handsomely for public engagements. He had a hit show on Broadway. There was no end to the windfall. On a whim one afternoon, he bought a $280 cashmere coat from Brooks Brothers. It was the most extravagant purchase of his life.

The following morning at the hotel, he and Beatrice had a falling out over the coat. He fell into a foul black mood, and by lunchtime, as she sat horrified across the table from him, begging him to stop, he began swilling glass after glass of champagne. By some accounts, he tore through seven or eight bottles in a short spell without pause. The American honeymoon was over. He headed for the Cort Theatre.

When Behan arrived outside the theater that night, security tried to persuade him not to enter, but he was the author of the play, and he was in no mood to be stopped. He entered the theater mid-production, stumbling down the aisle singing at the top of his lungs, much to the shock and amusement of the startled audience. The cast, realizing there was no way of avoiding the ensuing drama, invited him onto the stage to join them in a song, as Behan yelled out to the crowd, "Can you hear me? Can you hear me in the mezzanine? How about the balcony? I had a falling out with my wife—it lasted all day."

By the following morning, the papers had the headlines they were praying for. "Brendan Takes a Tumble from the Wagon" "Behan Dropped His Milk Glass." It was the beginning of the end for Behan. Over the next four years, he would fulfill every expectation of the stereotype he had hoped to avoid. He would never write another thing of worth.

During a hospital stay in Toronto the following year, where he was being held after collapsing after a drunken arrest, the doctor informed him that he had diabetes, and any continuation of alcohol consumption would be considered suicidal. But nothing was going to stop the juggernaut his life had become. The more he drank, the more press he received. Audiences flocked to see his show now in the hopes that they might witness the spectacle of the drunken author taking to the stage. He did not disappoint.

But behind the facade, Behan's demons were tearing him apart. There were reports of physical spousal abuse; he was accused of the attempted rape of a young editor in a hotel room; he took a young male lover by the name of Peter Arthurs; he fathered a child with a nineteen-year-old girl he had hired as a secretary. Beatrice stood by him through it all, defending him in public at every opportunity. She convinced him to return home to Dublin, thinking he was safer there. At least in Dublin she knew where he was most of the time, and who he was drinking with. But Behan would never again be content to stay in Dublin; he had tasted something in the freedom America afforded him that he couldn't find at home.

In late February 1963, Behan left for New York again, on a whim. He'd been drinking heavily and headed for the airport. This time he didn't even bother to tell his wife. On arriving in Manhattan, he booked himself into a roach motel. The management at the Algonquin had made it clear that they no longer wanted to see him on the premises. Not that he could have afforded it any longer. Many of his old haunts, dive bars used to every sort of degradation, turned him away also. He was a shell of a man on a suicidal rampage.

At some point, he wound up ensconced at the Chelsea Hotel, tended to by some kindhearted friends who were eager to try and nurse him back to health and keep him out of Bellevue psychiatric ward. Beatrice arrived by boat about a month later to see if she could help coax him to come back home. She carried with her a secret she feared might put him over the edge completely…she was two months pregnant with his child.

When she did eventually find the courage to tell Behan the news, he went straight to a lawyer and drew up a will leaving everything to Beatrice, then disappeared on another bender. Arthur Miller, who was staying at the Chelsea Hotel at the time, wrote of seeing Behan regularly outside, drunkenly holding court on the street to anyone who would stop to listen, "the vomit coming up and dripping on his tie as he joked and told stories and sung a few ditties."

Within weeks Beatrice returned to the room to find a naked, bloodied Behan almost catatonic. He'd had a seizure. He was stretchered out and taken to the intensive ward at New York University Hospital. Once awake, though, he would not be kept. He demanded booze. At one point he rambled into the cafeteria of the hospital and grabbed a pitcher of vinegar from a waitress filling table bottles, and he drank it straight down. Minutes later he was back on the street, delusional, half dead and drinking again.

Beatrice in a last-ditch attempt to save his life booked them tickets to sail back to Ireland on July 3rd. Surprisingly, probably knowing that his body would not hold up much longer, he went along amicably. Pete Arthurs, his longtime lover, showed up to say goodbye just before Brendan boarded the ship. "If it's a boy, maybe you'll name him after me…" Arthurs said, referring to

Brendan's impending fatherhood. It was the last time the two men would see each other.

As the *Queen Elizabeth* pulled out of New York Harbor, Beatrice recounted later, Behan stood quietly watching the skyline of the city he loved so much recede into the distance for what he knew in his heart would be the last time, then went to his cabin and began to drink.

Behan's daughter, Blanaid, was born in Dublin on November 24, 1963. Brendan died four months later, March 24, 1964.

Colin Broderick

# Charles R. Hale

Charles R. Hale was born, raised and educated in New York and is a descendant of New York City's Irish famine immigrants. His historically-themed essays have been published in literary magazines; his shows, including *The Musical History of the Lower East Side, New York City: A Shining Mosaic, Jazz and the City: The New York Connection* and *Crossing Boroughs* have been performed throughout the New York Metro, and he created and produced a film about the singer Judy Collins: *Walls: We Are Not Forgotten.* He is a co-founder of Artists Without Walls, an organization purposed to inspire, uplift and unite people and communities of diverse cultures through the pursuit of artistic achievement. In 2013, Hale was honored by the City University of New York for "Outstanding Service to New York and Irish America."

# Out of the Shadows: Giving Voice to the Scorned and Forgotten

Charles Ryder, one of the lead characters in Evelyn Waugh's *Brideshead Revisited*, a painter in civilian life who has become an officer in the British army during World War II, reaches a crisis point as the war grinds on. He says, "Here, at the age of thirty-nine I began to be old… I would go on with my job, but I could bring to it nothing more than acquiescence."

Like Ryder, I had a successful career, but my career, my dream, and I had grown tired together. Many years of therapy and self-analysis had turned into self-absorption. I tired of talking and interpreting my actions. That's when I began writing.

— —

I didn't start off as an Irish-American writer. How could I? I had only two links to Ireland: I confessed to Irish priests—Reilly, Reagan, and McCarthy—and Saint Patrick's Day, a one-day, unholy mess of Irish excess. Catholic schools, confraternity, Sunday Mass, Catholic Youth Organization basketball games, dances, and retreats reminded us, as if we could forget, that we were Catholic. My family names rang of Ireland—Kelly, Sullivan, Horrigan, and Lyons—and fourteen of my sixteen great-great-grandparents emigrated from Ireland to New York City, yet my ancestry remained shrouded in silence, secrets, and oblique remarks.

I was raised and educated in New York, but I knew little of my early New York ancestors. I assumed that they, like millions of immigrants, fled political and personal persecution, oppression, and hunger, and struggled to improve their family's lives. But when they died, their voices went with them. As each new wave of ancestors surged forth, each successive generation washed over the rest, leaving few traces of familial or cultural inheritance. For generations, it seems, my family suffered from a form of collective amnesia; it was better to forget.

While there was a dearth of ancestral and family stories, storytelling, which has been an integral part of Irish culture for centuries, was an important part of my youth. My father, Charlie, and his father, Grandpa Charlie, were inveterate storytellers. But other than my father's childhood escapades and Grandpa Charlie's stories of his life in the New York City fire department, family memories were rarely handed down. And to complicate matters, they were oral storytellers, not writers, and thus the stories, all the ordinary joys and sorrows of the earlier generations, went unrecorded and forgotten…all but one.

— —

"My father was working in the family butcher shop in Castleblayney when the trouble started, Charles," my maternal grandfather, Allie, said of his father, George Gorman. "A policeman entered the shop and started cuffin' him around. My father was only fifteen, but he didn't take guff from anyone. I'm afraid he responded…and then some. That night, in the winter of 1888, my father packed a bag and left for America. He never saw his family or Ireland again."

That was the only story that linked me directly to Ireland. There was talk that George had hit the officer with one of the butcher shop's implements, but I spent years researching that supposed event and found nothing. George Gorman was not spoken of with affection—my grandfather Allie and my grandfather's sister, Helen, described George as disputatious, vain, arrogant, unaffectionate, alcoholic, and opinionated—but I found no evidence that he had committed a heinous crime.

Over the years, however, I retained a degree of curiosity about George's travails, and eventually I made plans to travel to Ireland and Castleblayney, where I had arranged to meet

Castleblayney's unofficial historian and octogenarian, Jackie Byrnes.

My family and I, including my mother, Dorothy Gorman Hale, arrived in Dublin and drove north to Castleblayney, where we met Jackie. Within a few minutes, Jackie made it clear that he knew nothing of the butcher shop incident. "But I grew up next to the Gorman farm," he said. "I'll take you out there."

We drove a mile from town, turned onto a dirt road, and soon the old rundown farmhouse, which was used for storage by the current owner, appeared. My mother and Jackie walked into the house while my family and I walked the property. Soon we too entered the house, where my mother was silently standing in front of the fireplace. She stood still, staring, imagining a scene scripted over a century ago. And although she didn't express it as such, my mother appeared to be on a pilgrimage and was, at last, standing in front of a holy shrine. I waited, not knowing what she was feeling. I felt my mother's emotions gather.

"It's the first time I've ever felt my father was connected to something," she said. "All we knew was when he was a child, he lived a miserable existence on the streets of New York, but it was as if nothing or no one came before his childhood. I don't know why I feel better, but I do. And it's the first time I've ever felt warmth for my grandfather George. No one ever had anything nice to say about him, but now his reason for coming to America doesn't seem so important. I just feel better knowing there really is a link, a connection between my father, my grandfather, and Ireland."

Two days after visiting Castleblayney, we drove to Kinsale, a seaside community in the south of Ireland. That evening we entered a pub where a young musician was singing and playing a mandolin. Midway through his first set he began singing about a town where the songwriter had grown up, left, and finally revisited. "In my memory I will always see, the town that I have loved so well. Where our school played ball by the gas yard wall, and we laughed through the smoke and the smell."

The song, written by Phil Coulter, was the "Town I Loved So Well." As I listened, a powerful emotion held sway over me, but like my mother, I had difficulty ascribing meaning to what I was feeling.

I purchased a Dubliner's CD, which included Coulter's tune, and I listened to it over and over as we made our way up Ireland's Atlantic coast. I wandered through the grass-knitted dunes along the coast and down the lanes where whitewashed buildings with turf roofs dot the countryside. The music of the pubs, a pint of Guinness, the smell of turf fires hanging on a breeze, the dewy mist that hovers over the patchwork quilts, and Coulter's song aroused in me the need to belong, to be connected, not only to a community but also to an undiscovered past.

Many great philosophers have talked about the human need for connection. The great humanitarian Albert Schweitzer talked about how nature compels us towards mutual dependence, and how, in the fibers of our being, we bear within ourselves the solidarity of each other. Was that what I was feeling? Was that what I longed for?

— —

A few days after my return from Ireland, I drove to New York's Calvary Cemetery, the "Celtic Burial Ground," where many of my ancestors are buried. Are the roots of my existence intertwined and braided in the stories of those who are buried there? Could I unearth my ancestors' stories and take the first steps toward developing an awareness of the life forces and current of meaning for which I was searching? Could I unravel a tangle of shadows?

I began in New York City's archives, the libraries and the churches, where the outlines of my family's existence are recorded in the old worn pages. I walked the streets and listened for the voices that echo through the ages; I began to breathe from my ancestors' space and time. I soon realized that Ireland's Cliffs of Moher, rising from the sea, are awe inspiring, yet no more so than the man-made Brooklyn Bridge, born of Irish-American labor, which spans the East River. My family's farm in Castleblaney exerts a strong pull, but no more than the streets of Manhattan and Brooklyn, where my ancestors built the tunnels and buildings, swept the streets, and risked their lives protecting others.

While researching the life of my great-great-grandfather James Tobin, I found a *New York Times* article titled "Fatal Accident." On September 20, 1868, James Tobin, aged thirty-eight, was killed when the platform he was standing on plunged five stories. James was hauling bricks to the top of the building. As was often the case, the immigrant took the rottenest, most dangerous jobs. For this they were treated with scorn.

The Irish were mocked in caricatures that dehumanized them. Frederick Opper, a cartoonist for *Puck* magazine, drew a cartoon titled "American Gold," which depicts a group of Irish laborers at a work site. A number of the workers, particularly a laborer who is hauling bricks, as my ancestor James was, are drawn with apelike features, seemingly less than human. These hardworking immigrants struggled to put food on their family's tables, yet they were ridiculed and described with disdain.

On further research, I discovered that on August 29, 1884, a fire broke out in a three-story frame tenement in Brooklyn's Irishtown, the home of my great-great-grandparents Pierce and Ella Keating and their six children. A fire company arrived, but as firemen entered the home, they were driven back by smoke. A fireman was able to get into the apartment and, crawling on his hands and knees, made his way into the Keatings' rooms. He stumbled across the bodies of Pierce and one of his six children, Daniel, nine years old. The fireman was able to drag the Keatings from the building. Daniel survived; Pierce, aged forty-four, died a few days later.

I learned that Pierce's son, Pierce Jr., was no stranger to trouble. I discovered articles in the *Brooklyn Eagle,* Brooklyn's leading daily in the late nineteenth century, of Pierce's arrests while living on Raymond Street. He was arrested once on a morals charge and once for assaulting his sister. He served time in the Raymond Street Prison, known as the "Gothic Horror," located one block from the family home.

Like many immigrants, the Keatings were confined to a very small neighborhood, populated by poor Irish immigrants who lived in overcrowded wood-framed houses that were, more often than not, firetraps. Crime and public drunkenness were common occurrences. A week after my great-granduncle Pierce was incarcerated in 1885, the *Brooklyn Eagle* published an inspection report of the jail. The conditions, by today's standards, were shocking. Seven dungeons, or black holes, used for the discipline of unruly inmates, were all occupied. They were used for inmates who were "quarrelsome" and for those who had attempted to escape.

Surrounded by the chaos of everyday life, the Gormans, Keatings, Tobins, and many others struggled to survive, but when they died, their voices went with them. Now it's left to me, a descendant, to piece together ancestral shards, to gather an accumulation of yesterdays, and to map my ancestors' spirits and emotions with words. By writing, I return their voices; I change the tradition of silence and secrets that have kept my ancestors unknown and unrecorded.

Now, fifteen years after my family visited Castleblayney, I can still see my mother standing in front of the fireplace in communion with her father and grandfather and those who came before them. The expressiveness of her silence was more powerful than any words I can write or speak. But in that moment, in her silence, I began to understand the human need for connection—in all our joys and sufferings, we are of each other.

Why do I write? I write stories of tragedy and loss so that we feel the suffering; from that, we acquire empathy. I write to acknowledge the struggles of the dispossessed; from that, we learn tolerance. I write to preserve the stories; they serve as guides. I write so that we don't forget.

"You're growing up. And rain sort of remains on the branches of a tree that will someday rule the Earth. And it's good that there is rain. It clears the month of your sorry rainbow expressions, and it clears the streets of the silent armies...so we can dance."

## *Jim Carroll*

*(August 1, 1949–September 11, 2009)*

# Dan Barry

Dan Barry, a senior writer at *The New York Times*, was born in Queens, New York, and is a graduate of St. Bonaventure University and New York University. He shared a 1994 Pulitzer Prize as a member of an investigative team at the Providence Journal, and since then has twice been a nominated Pulitzer finalist. He is the author of *Pull Me Up: A Memoir*; *City Lights*, a collection of his "About New York" columns; *Bottom of the 33rd: Hope, Redemption, and Baseball's Longest Game*, which won the 2012 PEN/ESPN Award for Literary Sportswriting; *The Boys in the Bunkhouse: Servitude and Salvation in the Heartland*; and *This Land: America, Lost and Found*, a collection of his national columns, published in September 2018.

# Last Words

Frank McCourt was said to be ill, quite ill, the news shared soft and prayerful among the small clutches of New York writers and artists who gathered at this Irish event or that Irish pub. It was hard to hear and harder to believe, so deeply did Frank provide the pulse to the group's core embrace of possibility. A high school teacher who measured his moments, writing, rewriting, re-rewriting—and then delivering a work for the ages, a memoir that slipped the cuffs of ethnic relegation.

Who among us has not wished authorship of the book's immortal second paragraph:

"When I look back on my childhood I wonder how I survived at all. It was, of course, a miserable childhood: the happy childhood is hardly worth your while. Worse than the ordinary miserable childhood is the miserable Irish childhood, and worse yet is the miserable Irish Catholic childhood."

Now our friend and mentor, our great champion of encouragement, was very ill, the prospect of his absence shadowing our days. I did what we do when we don't know what else to do: I sent Frank a get-well card disguised as a carefree note; a promise of prayers that made no mention of God or prayer. I thanked him again for his many kindnesses to me, and expressed the hope of getting together soon.

The absence of a response from Frank before his death, in 2009, did not bother me. I comforted myself with a letter he had sent me several years earlier, after he had read a manuscript of my own memoir, *Pull Me Up*. In the envelope he had included a kind blurb on one piece of paper and, on another, a personal note that for the first time gave me permission to at least begin thinking of myself as a writer.

Before receiving Frank's letter, I was a newspaper reporter—

not even a journalist but a reporter, and I am proud to call myself one still. To hell with "Get me rewrite"; I want to be the one calling in facts from the scene of a fire—and the one at a newsroom keyboard, arranging those facts into a deadline story that trembles, the flames seen, the smoke inhaled, the heat of loss felt deep beneath the skin.

But to declare myself a writer? What presumption. The clattering ghosts of my antecedents, the Barrys and Minogues, the farmers and clerks, the daily tipplers and professional sufferers, would keen in chorus over my assured damnation for having committed that grievous Irish-American sin: to forget one's place.

Then arrived this piece of paper. A limitless hallway pass, an unrestricted license—a diploma, bestowing upon me the unremitting sorrows and ephemeral joys of the writer's life. All written out and signed in the inky scratches of Frank McCourt, as fine to my eyes as the calligraphy of any Columban monk.


After having written thousands of newspaper columns and stories over a thirty-five-year career, I struggle with specifics. A few stories stand out, particularly those from the immediate aftermath of 9/11; when unburied from the coping mechanisms of the mind, that day becomes today. But most stories feel like small tributaries into the narrative ever-flow of the human condition. A planning and zoning committee meeting in Connecticut blends into a mob hit in Rhode Island, into a City Hall news conference with a jaw-jutting Mayor Giuliani, into hurricanes blowing through Louisiana bayous and migrant workers toiling in Minnesota beet fields, the bumps and grinds of a retired burlesque queen reunion in Baraboo, Wisconsin, the police shootings of unarmed young black men, a gobsmacking presidential election.

But a distinct point of personal departure came with a routine assignment I received back in April 1997, in my early years at *The New York Times*. From out of nowhere, a writer about whom I knew very little had just won the Pulitzer Prize for biography, an honor entitling any recipient to cancel all obligations for a week of hedonic celebration. But no: This writer was keeping a speaking engagement at a Long Island high school in distant Suffolk County, about five miles from where I had grown up.

The writer, of course, was Frank McCourt. He won a Pulitzer Prize on a Monday, and on that Wednesday he went to an auditorium in Bay Shore to engage a squirming, shimmering mass of high school students in the subject of writing.

I introduced myself to Frank, and we talked for a while in the teacher's lounge, the obligatory spread of Entenmann's and muffins laid out before us. Amid all the small-town exhilaration —we have with us a Pulitzer Prize winner, newly minted!—he maintained an air of wise detachment, as if his miserable Irish Catholic childhood had conditioned him not to get too ahead of himself, for somewhere, surely, there lurked comeuppance and heartbreak. He understood that honors and awards were as impermanent as pastries.

Then it was time for this white-haired retired schoolteacher of sixty-six to speak. From the moment he took the stage, Frank demonstrated his muscle-memory ability to mesmerize a roomful of students, no matter that many of them were caught in the throes of disadvantaged youth. They fell silent as he spoke of his own challenged circumstances as a youth in Brooklyn and in Ireland, where there was nothing lyrical or twee about the lice and alcoholism and deprivation.

"I learned the significance of my own insignificant life," Frank said, before encouraging the students to recognize the storytelling power of their own lives, to see the epic possibilities of their Long Island existence.

When he finished, the teenagers stomped their feet in

affirmation. Sitting to the side, pen and notebook in hand, I may well have joined in. With his sideways humor and entrancing brogue, this Frank McCourt had given me encouraging consent. You may fall on your ass, Barry. Make that: You will fall on your ass.

But go for it. Explore the significance of your own insignificant life.

McCourt's words more than followed me; they goaded me, echoing all those boyhood taunts for being afraid to climb a tree, dive into a lake, eat a worm. So, between newspaper assignments that included two years as the City Hall bureau chief during the Giuliani administration, I began tapping out bits of stories, aborted starts at some unformed personal narrative with no beginning, middle, end, or thought. Then I wrote a manuscript for a novel about—get this—a melancholy Irish-American newspaper reporter. (The manuscript remains locked away in an undisclosed location, not worth even the matchstick to set it afire.) Then I got cancer.

Cancer, like deadlines and executions, concentrates the mind. But at the same time that it threatens to cut your oxygen intake forever, the disease also gives oxygen to every hoary generalization, including the one about having your life flash before your eyes. In my case, the very real prospect of death was the unspoken subtext of the daily conversation, with oncologists averting their eyes while delivering the next discouraging test result, and the next. My life didn't so much flash before me as it flickered like the silent home movies of my childhood that were once cast upon a screen of basement plywood. One reel would unspool through the projector of my mind, a long-ago Christmas morning, a Halloween gathering, a birthday party, a First Holy Communion. Remember the blue suit? The white boutonniere? The formality befitting an eight-year-old boy feigning comprehension of transubstantiation? My godfather gave me twenty-five dollars.

During regular five-day residencies at Memorial Sloan-Kettering Cancer Center, I was leashed to a beeping IV pole while a Drano-like concoction clear as poteen dripped into me in metronomic Hail Mary drops. As I took that pole for woozy shuffles through the forbidding halls — it was the stoic Rogers to my shuffling Astaire — I contemplated my inconsequential and threatened life. A New York Irish-American life.

I had never before reflected so deeply on how the South Shore of Long Island, which I had spent decades fleeing, had influenced me. Now, thanks to Frank McCourt, I began to see my piece of the island in a larger context: as a place where the Depression children of New York City brick and asphalt, sons who had fought in Normandy and Inchon, daughters who had held family and the home front together, found grass. Just grass. It might be a small swath of green, no more than two car lengths, but it was theirs, and they cultivated it, manicured it, and then, sitting in the shade of an open garage with a can of Rheingold in hand, they watched as the lazy sway of a lawn sprinkler cast rainbows upon their grass.

I inherited their Cagney strut and arrogance. Their transposed *ois* and *ers*, *terlet* for toilet, *goil* for girl. Their blue-collar sensibility that nothing in life falls off a truck; you have to work for it. Their enduring identification with the unattainable city of their birth, with Brooklyn and the Bronx, Washington Heights and the Lower East Side, and the nagging sense that they would always be the Dead End Kids down at the docks, cooking mickeys over a fire while the swells danced in a glass-encased penthouse far above them. As for the poverty and war endured, the broken families, the alcoholism, the grieving? Never discussed, never acknowledged. Hardships were stipulated, given voice only through the hiss of a cracked-open can of beer. If a telltale sigh escaped, signaling a suppressed memory threatening to surface—say, of my father being tied to a lamppost as his parents drank—his neighbor expressed solidarity, or understanding, or even love, with a simple:

'Nother beer there, Gene?

The Long Island amen.

Our fathers were hardly the Cú Chulainns of Suffolk County. Some harbored racist feelings, and some drank too much, and some beat their children, and some left their families in body or spirit. They were flawed men, saved usually by their less-flawed wives. But rather than dismiss them as Cheever caricatures, living out soulless existences in ticky-tacky suburban tracts, I now saw these men and women as honorable—even, at times, heroic. The low-rung accountants and back-office workers, ties askew and faces drawn as they belched out of the saunalike Long Island Rail Road cars and into the muggy August nights. The grease-streaked gas-station attendants and Grumman mechanics, the foot-weary clerks coming back from the Macy's at the South Shore Mall or the Woolworth's in the Sunset City shopping center.

Confined to an Upper East Side cancer hospital bed, too ill to read or watch television or even take that beeping IV pole for a spin, I closed my eyes to still the dizziness and heard their *er*s and *oi*s again. And whatever had previously been my arrogant measure of a life's worth, it now came down to this: They tried.

With nothing to do but retch and think, my chemo-haze contemplations drilled deeper into the core question summoned in the encroaching shadow of mortality. Who am I? Or: Who was I? Down, down, my thoughts went, to places dark as peat, and I imagined their first meeting in the mid-1950s, in the midlands of Brooklyn, at some repressed church dance, in the basement of Our Lady of Chance Encounters.

He was Irish-American and Nelson Eddy handsome with

blond hair Brylcreem-slick, certain that he was smarter than anyone in the room but without the credentials, having finished high school at night, then three years in the Army, then work, work, work, cold-calling on Wall Street. This was Gene, a New York Depression child through and through, sharp, funny, charming to women, distrusting of power, damaged.

And she? Not yet eighteen and still new to this roiling county of Kramden-like kings. At fifteen, she had left her Third World country, left a small Galway farm in a place called Gortmucca, which in Irish means "field of pigs," carrying little more than a brown-leather autograph book containing the farewells of friends and siblings. ("Though the hills and vales divide us, and together we cannot be, whenever you think of old Ireland, always think of me.") Her mother was five years dead and her dying father was unable to rear children, so an aunt who worked as a silver-polishing domestic in a Long Island mansion had paid her fare. Now she was no longer Nora. She was Noreen, one of the girls in the typing pool at Equitable Life, pretty, stylish, smoking cigarettes, not yet violating the Pioneer's Pledge to abstain from alcohol, curious about what comes next.

Gene, Noreen. Noreen, Gene.

They courted, married, set up home in Queens, had their first child of four children, not counting a stillborn and a couple of miscarriages. Though neither knew yet how to drive, they moved to a lower-middle-class neighborhood in Long Island and established a home in which the language spoken was an Irish-American lingual blend.

Here we had the father, raging against the Nixonian crown, feeling acutely the oppression of the system—though he, at least, had broken free of that lamppost leash to have his own plot of grass: an abrupt backyard where he brooded, drank, listened to Irish music, and found fleeting joy in the glide of a passing bird. He did not gather his children to recite Yeats or Kavanagh, but he did read aloud those Irish-American newspaper bards, Breslin and Hamill, and he did watch the comic actor Gleason on *The Honeymooners*, identifying with the common-man struggle and the inside Irish joke that life is best lived with the certainty of tragedy stipulated.

And here we had the mother, conditioned by now to distract her troubled husband and worried children with stories. Though the harsh Long Island argot was slowly rubbing away her brogue, she still had the gift, summoning the curlicue imagery and sideways observations in the manner of her parents and grandparents, back in that field of pigs, weaving tales of magical holy wells and oddball bachelor farmers, her hearth now a muted television. Now, instead of child-snatching fairies—*Come away, O human child*—she displaced the household dysfunction with, say, the epic of having gone to Shop Rite to buy a quart of milk and what the woman in front of her was buying and what kind of mother is that anyway who's buying Cap'n Crunch for her children, and you should have seen how the clerk worked her gum, and the assistant manager was hovering about, a very important man, for sure, given the nine pens he had in his wrinkly shirt's pocket protector....

As I received the chemotherapy that would keep illness at bay for a few years but not forever, I thought of my mother, dead less than a year—of cancer, of course. Her cigarettes had been part of her storytelling performance, their enveloping blue smoke a kind of stagecraft, a hazy, gossamer curtain that briefly separated her rapt children from the reality of alcoholism and depression and considerable financial stress.

Two working-class nobodies, my parents, their aspirations now modified to a deserved retirement that would never come, toiling in anonymity in the middle of an often-maligned appendage to Gotham. I realized their profound significance.

Then again, you can so easily romanticize your own narrative.

Was my father that damaged? Was my mother that good? Christ, am I also sentimentalizing my own goddam cancer?

This fretting passed. Here I was in my sickbed, and there I was in that small backyard on an autumn Sunday, the two of them warmed by sweaters and also the beers kept in a cooler ever-close at hand. The Clancy Brothers and Tommy Makem were singing our family soundtrack from a cassette player or that Irish radio station in the Bronx. It was always the 23rd of June, and the birds were singing in yon bush, and at the foot of the hill there was a neat little still, and oh for the love of Peggy Gordon, and Eileen Aroon, and, yes, Nancy Whiskey. All by the rising of the moon, in the ranks of the men of the West, and the Croppy boy, and poor Kevin Barry, was I related, another martyr for old Ireland, another murder for the crown. I was twelve, listening to songs of war and misogyny and alcohol abuse, but what I heard were the possibilities of story, and the nimbleness of language.

The liquor scattered over Tim.

Tim revives, see how he rises

Timothy rising from the bed

"Whirl your whiskey around like blazes

*Th'anam 'on diabhal,* do ye think I'm dead?"

And Lord, there was resurrection through the holy waters of whiskey, of chemo. If I ever slip this tightening noose, I thought, I will write of the significant insignificance.

A year or so after Frank McCourt's death, the New York writers and artists gathered once again at some Irish event, and in attendance this night was Frank's lovely and witty widow, Ellen McCourt. After the hellos and how-are-yous, Ellen asked: Dan, you wrote to Frank shortly before he died, didn't you?

Yes.

Well, he wrote back to you, but for some reason it was never delivered. Shall I send it on to you?

Yes.

Please.

A few days later, I received a handwritten letter from the late, great Frank McCourt, as if ink instead of whiskey had scattered over him. Yes, he wrote, he would love to get together sometime. And so we do. Again and again.

"I don't give a damn about reviews. What I like to read are royalty checks."

*Mickey Spillane*

*(March 9, 1918–July 17, 2006)*

# Seamus Scanlon

Seamus Scanlon was born and raised in Galway; he emigrated to New York in 2005. He has written a trilogy of plays dealing with war in Northern Ireland (1969–1999): *The McGowan Trilogy*. He has also written *The Blood Flow Game* and *Three-Nil*. He has had his work produced by the Cell Theater Company in Manhattan and by the Poor Mouth Theatre company in the Bronx. He lives in Forest Hills, Queens.

# Outside It's New York

Inside it's Galway

Home of Nora Barnacle, the Poor Clares, the Prom, Liam Mellows, the Connaught Rangers, An Réalt, An Taibhdhearc, Druid, the Quiet Man, the Galway Races, Lord Haw Haw, Gentian Hill, the Bish (Academy of Latin and Street Fighting), The Rattlesnakes, Rahoon Cemetery, the Apache Laffeys (who never laughed), the Great Fire of Galway, the Great Southern, Le Graal, Scoil an Linbh Íosa, Cemetery Cross.

Inside me lives: the sharp stink sting in the back of my throat from McDonagh's Fertilizer Plant; the deep canals; the heavy vibration of diesel engines of Atlantic-bound trawlers in the gray dawn; rain without end; heavy black clouds coming in from the Atlantic; the Burren shrouded in mist across Galway Bay; the crack of rifle fire at Renmore Barracks in the mornings; heavy slow goods trains passing alongside me as I walked the military path into Ceannt Station; the Corrib in full spate carrying all before it—boys who wanted to be girls, girls with ripe pregnant bellies, women fecund with malignancies, and men with black angels hovering above them.

Inside motion and emotion flows through me.

Inside it's Mervue.

Lithe, lean cheetahs race down Emmet Avenue. Boot-boys beautiful. Balletic street-fighting kings. My mother fixes them up. When they call to the door, I just nod and show them in. They stride past me. We all know the routine. I can smell the danger off them. And something else.

My mother says put on the kettle, boil some water.

I am doing it already.

She takes out the medical instruments she carried from

230

London to open TB wards in Dublin, then to Inis Oírr, then to Carraroe where Brendan Behan asked her out, then to Old Mervue, where I fought my way through the deep to make it to shore battered and bruised.

Inside, it's Nurse McGowan.

In the bare front room drops of blood fall at her feet and the wooden floorboards eat them up. Her instruments are laid out on the table. She jokes with them as she waits for the hot water. She never jokes with me. I wonder about it. I bring the kettle in. She pours the water into the stainless-steel bowl and drops in the scissors, the tweezers, and needles she uses to extract splinters of glass (from bottles) and metal slivers (from iron bars and rusty blades). She pours Dettol into the bowl. The water goes milky white. She deftly cleans and sutures. I stand beside her. I am number-one assistant surgeon. The boot-boy acolytes watch me from across the room. I am safe from them in here.

Inside is it won't kill you

My mother finishes up. They are mild and meek before her. They are boys only, though they have the urban wild gene deep inside them.

She says, Heat up the kettle again to me.

I am number-one tea boy.

She dries off her instruments and wraps them. She makes the tea. The boot boys in their parallels and Doc Martens and scrubbed faces and scalped hairlines hold the mugs. They eat a full packet of Thin Arrowroot between them. My favorite. I watch closely their high cheekbones and their bright eyes and facial scars and shorn skulls. They get ready to leave. Ma checks the injury again of the latest Mervue warrior.

You will live, she says.

But she was wrong.

Inside, it's German shepherds

**231**

The Mervue boot boys never attack me. They chase me sometimes. For practice. For fun. For pure pain. Their metal cleats striking the wet paths marked out the distance behind me. I was fine-tuned to echolocation before long. They do shout out as they run up on me. I hear their easy breathing behind me. Then they just run past me.

Come on granny. Move your arse.

They run off ahead. They laugh. Their German shepherds stride beside them tethered to their wrists with long chains that trail along the wet roadway.

A German shepherd attacked me once in Mervue. I vaulted the connecting garden wall of two houses. He was annoyed. He cut me. He bit me. He had beautiful teeth. Like I used to have. I was doing God's work collecting church envelopes. It did not save me. I knew then it was a cod. The God-believing hocus-pocus. I was twelve. I said fuck that. I threw the envelopes into the wild Galway wind.

Inside is a Comanche.

Every summer the tinkers camped near us. Their hobbled piebald ponies moved slowly down Emmet Avenue like a herd of automatons lurching forward. Their front legs were tethered with cloth strips. Their eyes stared straight ahead. A deep compulsion to walk drove them. I stepped down from the path. I walked beside them. I patted the lead one. I carried a homemade bow. The arrows I cut from the yew trees that grew in Mervue Woods. I flattened the metal caps from mineral bottles into primitive and jagged arrowheads using a lump hammer. I fired them from the backyard over the roof hoping to hit the soft, pale skin of the hard boys who ran wild.

Inside is Callow Lake.

Where boys swam before me. They jumped off the high drop rocks and shouted, "Banzai" before they hit the surface. Heavy dark rain clouds rolled across the lake pushed down from the black mountain of Cullneachtain. Sheets of warm rain struck the lake surface as I tried to row across. The rain hid a lot. When the rain lashed me in fierce gusts, I stood up and, with arms uplifted, let the rain clean me. Bless me father for I have sinned. For I have not died. I lay on the boat slips of Callow Lake until the rising tide lifted me clear and I floated all night watching the stars. Maybe I could be a writing star. Not really. Maybe I could be brave. Not really. Maybe someone would see me. Not really.

Inside I am blooded.

On the slick road outside Kiltimagh on the way home to Swinford from my first abortive disco outing, the Volkswagen Beetle swerved off the slick road into the high embankment. My cousin Sean braked too quickly. His girl Bernie sat beside him in the passenger seat, a cigarette in her slender fingers. In the back a girl slammed into me—her head cracked off mine. Her teeth opened a cut over my eye. I still have the scar. It hurts on cold nights still. I am a total romantic. Not really.

She screamed.

Bernie said fuck!

Blood drops fell slowly onto the warm seats. I was blooded forever. Ten years later Sean was buried in Swinford Cemetery. Cancer ate him up. I miss him still.

Inside is wander lust

My father tried to escape at nights. He strained against me at the front door. 3:00 a.m. and all's not well.

He said I will have to get rough with you.

Inside I laughed. I could throw him across the room. He was skin and bone. He was demented. His hand was tight around my wrist. His eyes were looking beyond me. He was on a mission. He was hardwired wander-wise. Up and out to the railway station. He thought he still worked there. I relented.

I said okay, I will drive you.

He nodded. I dressed in a minute. I was as good at it now as the firemen in Fr. Burke Road. We got into the Opel Vectra. Perfect precision engineering. Unlike Da's. There was a one-inch, high-silvered, colored angel on the top of the dashboard. It was called a parking angel. You wound it at the back when you needed parking. Its wings lifted in mechanical slow motion.

What is that? Da asked every time.

An angel. You know heaven. Where you are going soon.

Am I?

Sure.

Okay.

I drove down Lough Atalia Avenue, then via Moneenageisha Cross, and Lough Atalia Road to the docks. I parked for a minute and lowered the windows. Sometimes he got out. Tonight he just watched the berthed trawlers three abreast moving slowly with the tide, the gunwales hitting against each other cushioned by the car and tractor tires hanging over the edge.

Okay?

He nodded. We drove around Eyre Square where I used to lie in the sun on hot summer days before the corruption of life soiled me. I am more fun in person. Maybe. The stationmaster shook hands with Da. He knew the score.

He told Da he had a day off.

You can manage so?

The stationmaster nodded. I nodded at him in thanks. Nodding is the equivalent of a bear hug, Galway-wise.


Outside it's New York
Inside it's Irish stories.
Outside New York assails me.
Inside Galway saves me.

# Oscar Wilde

*(October 16, 1854–November 30, 1900)*

No Irish author in history lent himself so fully to the pursuit of celebrity as Oscar Wilde. Wilde's life story reads like a precursor to the modern day obsession with self-promotion. His novel *A Picture of Dorian Gray* can be viewed as a haunting premonition of the dangers of narcissism and an eerie foreboding of the age of the selfie.

He was born Oscar Fingal O'Flahertie Wills Wilde, on 16 October 1854, and raised at No. 1 Merrion Square, Dublin. His mother, Lady Jane Wilde, was an eccentric Irish revolutionary poet of the time who ran a salon for artists. As a boy, Oscar attended many of these gatherings. His father, Sir William Wilde, was Dublin's most famous eye and ear surgeon; he was also considered something of a world-class scoundrel—a notorious drinker and womanizer who fathered three children out of wedlock.

Oscar attended the elite Portora Royal School in Enniskillen. While at Portora, Oscar's younger sister Isola died of a fever (possibly meningitis). Her death profoundly affected Oscar and informed practically everything he ever wrote. In 1881 he penned the poem "Requiescat" in her memory.

After Portora, Oscar attended Trinity on a Royal scholarship, and after Trinity, Oxford. He was a sight to behold, strolling around campus, at six foot two, with his long flowing hair, silk pants, and knee britches. He was deeply immersed in the new aesthetic movement—a school of thought that favored the adoration of beauty in physical objects, "art for art's sake." It was a school of thought that bore a stark contrast to the stuffy Victorianism of English society at the time; a school of thought that challenged ingrained notions of morality, spirituality, and sexuality.

In understanding Oscar Wilde, it is important to understand just how rebellious this new aesthetic movement was considered at the end of the nineteenth century. At one point Wilde received fierce criticism at Oxford for stating, "I find it harder and harder every day to live up to my blue china."

Oscar's dramatic physical presence brought him to the attention of the producers of the Gilbert and Sullivan production *Patience*. *Patience* was a hugely successful comic opera in London at the time. It lampooned the aesthetic movement with its themes of vanity, pretension, and superficiality. The producers, fearing an American audience was not quite up to speed, hired Oscar Wilde, the aesthetic movement's most visible representative, to visit America ahead of the production as a way of drumming up publicity.

A twenty-seven-year-old Oscar Wilde arrived in New York on January 2, 1882. In an interview conducted with Wilde before he disembarked the ship, a reporter from *The Sun* (New York), quoted him as saying, "I was very much disappointed in the Atlantic Ocean." It was a quote that was to establish Oscar as an arrogant, pretentious fop before he even set foot on American soil. His silk cloak, knee britches, and shoulder-length hair made for wonderful copy.

Over the next year Wilde toured America lecturing. By all accounts it was not a forum he was particularly talented at. *The New York Times* called his lectures "boring, monotonous and wearisome." But the general public couldn't get enough of him. Oscar embraced the controversy. On a trip to one of the country's most majestic natural wonders, he quipped, "I was disappointed with Niagara. Most people must be disappointed with Niagara," He traipsed around the midwest in knee socks twirling an ivory cane, and fired off witty one-liners to the press wherever he went. His theatrical air of condescension and eccentric mode of dress made him an easy caricature at a time when photography was rare. Drawings of Wilde from the time almost always depicted him holding a flower, or in many cases dressed as a flower, a not-so-subtle jab at his effeminate demeanor. Wilde reveled in it all.

Back in New York, Wilde arranged to have his portrait taken by Napoleon Sarony, one of the most famous photographers of the time. Sarony photographed Wilde decked in all his finery, reclining on a fur-draped chaise lounge. The portrait did more to cement the legend of Oscar Wilde than anything he had written up to that point in his life.

Wilde left America in December 1882 a wealthy celebrity.

There followed a period of relative calm in his life. He married and had two sons. He was a devoted and loving father. Then he met a young man by the name of Robert Ross who awakened in Wilde the potential of his homosexuality.

Over the next decade Wilde would produce his most memorable work. In 1890 Lippincott's magazine published "The Picture of Dorian Gray." The work was vilified for its thinly veiled homosexual undertones. Wilde was already skating on thin ice at a time in England when homosexuality was ruled a crime and punishable by imprisonment. Wilde could not resist the temptation to poke the bear. His newfound sexual freedom fueled a flurry of essays, short stories, and plays.

In 1891, thirty-six-year-old Wilde met and fell in love with a twenty-year-old Lord Alfred Douglas. It was a relationship that would devastate him personally and professionally. The two men started living together in a series of London hotels. Wilde explained to his wife that he needed privacy away from the family to write. But he underestimated the patience of the Victorian society he mocked so gloriously in plays such as *Lady Windermere's Fan, An Ideal Husband* and *The Importance of Being Earnest.*

Lord Alfred's father, the Marquess of Queensbury, enraged with his son's relationship with Wilde, accused the author of sodomy. In 1895 Wilde, against the advice of his friends, took Queensbury to court to defend his name against libel. It was a dangerous move on Wilde's part, but he would not be swayed. Wilde's public defense of his reputation had the effect of exposing the true nature of his relationship with Alfred. In defending his good name, he practically signed his own death warrant.

On April 5th, 1895, Wilde was arrested and charged with the crime of sodomy. The publicity he had sought for so long now turned against him. He was shunned by society. His name was stripped from playbills. His belongings were sold off at auction to pay his debts. On May 25th, he was convicted of gross indecency and sentenced to two years of hard labor.

In prison he wrote a letter of anger and directed toward his lover, Lord Alfred Douglas. (The letter, titled De Profundis, was published five years after Wilde's death.)

Prison destroyed Oscar Wilde. On the night he was released after two years' hard labor, he left England under an alias, never to return. He was broke and destitute, his name destroyed. His last letters revealed a man dealing with profound loneliness, poverty, hunger, and pain. Doctors operated on an abscess in his ear that went untreated while he was in prison, but Wilde was not strong enough to mount the fight needed to regain his health. His spirit had been shattered, his heart broken.

Oscar Wilde died in a hotel room in Paris in November 1900. He was forty-six years old. Found amid the few possessions he had managed to keep with him through those tumultuous last years was an envelope containing a lock of hair. The inscription on the envelope read: "My Isola's Hair."

Colin Broderick

# Brian O'Sullivan

Brian O'Sullivan emigrated to New York from County Kerry in 1988. He has worked construction for almost thirty years in Manhattan. In 2013 he published his debut memoir, *Butcher a Hog*.

# Plastering Over the Words in New York

I was forty years of age. I was locked up inside the madhouse below in the now demolished Saint Vincent's Hospital, on Twelfth Street. I was having a hard time verbalizing what was going on with me, so a doctor suggested I write down whatever it was that was bothering me. I'd nothing to lose, so I gave it a shot. About a week later, the very same doctor asked to have a gander at the scrawl. He read it intently. He says to me after, I had a distinct way of writing, and that his gut feeling was that at some point I would sit down and write a book. What? I'd shown him the depths of my insides, and the best he could come up with was this shite? Me, a plasterer, whose only desire in life was not to do shoddy work. I fucked him out of it, and got an injection in the arse to quell me down, on account of it.

Turns out the cunt was right, though. Four hellish years later, I did indeed sit down and write a novel. 'Twas an act of desperation. You see, I'd spent the guts of the twelve previous months in various other madhouses throughout the city, on account of constantly taking suicidal amounts of pills and drinking copious amounts of rubbing alcohol. I was in a kinda horrific pain of a classification that'd make it impossible even for Freud himself to wrap his head around. It got so bad at one point that they were going to send me to a state facility, they were. They didn't though. No, they gave me twelve shots of electric-shock therapy instead. A week after the treatments, I was home in my bed, and some sorta episode came over me. I couldn't breathe. I couldn't walk. I couldn't talk. 'Twas all on account of an episode that had occurred in Ireland, thirty-five years prior. I crawled inta the living room to try and call 911. I didn't do it though. No, I opened up a laptop and started

241

writing about the madness in my brain. The next day I went to the Coffeepot, on Forty-ninth and Ninth, and kept going. Even though I wasn't the best at the old typing, I knew right then and there that morning that I'd finish some sorta book. On top of that, I felt genuinely alive for the first fucking time in my life. For years all kinds of doctors and therapists had been asking me what it was I thought was wrong with me. As I said before, not even the great Freud himself would've been able to describe it. The writing changed everything though. I'd found my voice. Being the most introverted, isolated cunt of a human being I know, 'twas a miraculous turnaround.Turned out writing the book was the easy part, though. I even started to write another one. I got halfway there. I lived in Hell's Kitchen at the time, and I was going to twelve-step meetings about the place. There was no shortage of writers at them. I started to show the work to some select few of them with very high self-esteem. I got nothing but encouragement and praise. I kept going at it. Events unfolded, though that put the blinkers on it fairly rapidly, and I took a two-year hiatus from the laptop on account of it. You see, the word "agent" came inta the equation. I hadn't a fucking clue what the people were on about. I was told I'd need to get one though, so I started to do a bit of research. I found out fairly fast what the story was. Everyone and their mother was looking to get one. What chance did I stand? Still, I had written what I was told was a fairly good book, so I had some kinda leverage. Getting the cunts to read it was near impossible, though. I must've sent out a coupla hundred query letters. A fairly well-known Irish-American "agent" got back to me. He told me I had a unique voice but he couldn't represent me on account of his currently representing another Irish junkie author. He gave me a few tips and we left it at that. Then the "agent" boy who represents your man who wrote *Running With Scissors* got back to me as well. He told me he liked the voice but it got lost somewhere along the way. I got a few more tips but that was me fucked again. As for the rest of them, 'twas nothing but a fucking nightmare dealing with them, it was. Send me this, send me that! Sorry, not for me! Rejection-rejection-rejection! I hafta admit to being very highly insulted on more than a few occasions, I must. What the fuck can you do just? I came up with a solution, though, that fairly rapidly put an end to the nonsense. You see, the last query letter I sent was to one out in Brooklyn. On her website she stated in her bio that she liked to snuggle up by the fire on a cold winter's evening and read something intriguing. Well, I sent her something to be intrigued about.

It went as follows:

> Dear Agent,
> I'm sending you a bit of a manuscript. I am aware in your submission guidelines that you do state that you require a bit of a bio, and some kinda synopsis along with the manuscript. I apologize for not sending them in advance, the reason being is I can't be bothered my arse to do so. So if you would be so kind as to forgo this omission and just go ahead and read the fucking thing, it will relieve me of much aggravation. If it intrigues you in any way what, please contact me at the address I have given below, and maybe we can talk business. On the other hand, however, if you think it's a heap of shite, do me a favor and throw it inta that fire of yours and burn it.
> Yours very sincerely,
> Brian O'

Needless to say, I haven't heard back from her yet. I got a good bit of frustration out though. Fuck the "agents"! I gave up. I threw in the towel and had the fucking thing self-published.

I was getting a bit of disability at the time on account of being mad, and it was accommodating the writing rightly. I had plenty of time on my hands to write, and enough money to fill the stomach. I pulled a stupid cunt of a move, though. Yeah, I went back to plastering in the union. There were some very serious repercussions on account of it. You see, plastering and sobriety has, and never will be a good match for me. Not a chosen profession, for one; plus factor in drugs and beer all over the place and you get the picture. So needless to say, after a very brief space of time, I relapsed. The writing went out the window as well that very same day I picked up, and another three years of sobriety went down the shitter. Once again I was fucked.

The family at home in Ireland didn't seem to mind my having written a book too much. I did get the old "It's a heap of shite" line from a couple of the sisters, but other than that there didn't seem to be any great animosity. "Renowned arts editor" Cahir O'Doherty wasn't long inadvertently changing all that though.... He called me of a Monday evening all excited. He'd read the book and he told me 'twas a great read. He then informed me that he wanted to do a two-page article in the *Irish Voice*. Not alone that, but he wanted it to go in the midsummer edition that would be in circulation for two weeks. He told me he only did this a few times a year. Fuck it, why not? He'd caught me off-guard though. You see, I'd held back in the book about what had gone on back in the day. I did this very purposely so as to not offend anyone. So Cahir basically says to me, You've written a fantastic book, so now please tell me who the fuck are you? I told him the truth just, and he published it. A coupla weeks later some boy named Conor from *Kerry's Eye* called. He asked me if he could do an article as well...he was going to shoot for the front page. Go for it I says to him. I remember thinking it kinda odd that he didn't interview me, but passed it no heed just. I wasn't thinking straight, though. A week later the article got published. It didn't make the front page, but it may as well on account of the uproar it caused. Conor had basically just

cut and pasted O'Doherty's piece and then juiced it up some...
meaning he sensationalized the shite out of it. "Kerry Writer
Takes America by Storm" I believe was the headline. 'Twas
news to me if he had, because "Kerry Writer" was over here in
America, plastering like a cunt in the United Nations building
on East Forty-second. I mentioned there I wasn't thinking
straight. I have a very good reason for saying it. You see, my
mother reads *Kerry's Eye* religiously. She didn't take too kindly
to the content of the piece (went to school with bruises, don't
tell anyone what happened, mother abandons her son—few
snippets of that kinda nature). The sisters were on the blower
right away. How could you have done this to her? What kind
of cruel person are you? I eventually stopped picking up. I was
disowned on account of it. To top that off my partner, Vivian,
and a six-year-old granddaughter were sent to Coventry as well.
What are you gonna do?

I used to cochair a Friday-night men's twelve-step meeting
with a good friend of mine Rick, in Hell's Kitchen. Myself
and himself became fairly close, and we spent manys a night
bullshitting in coffee shops. An interesting character now he
is. He's inta film and documentaries, and makes a living at it.
He doesn't toot his horn about it though. A very humble man
just. Anyway, I'd asked him to read the manuscript before I had
it published. He'd put me off a few times on account of him
having very traumatic instances of reading other people's work
in the past. He has high self-esteem you see, so if he reads it
you get the truth, and he doesn't like hurting people's feelings.
Eventually though he caved in and read it. He texted me at page
three, and says to me this is brilliant. He mentioned to me that
his wife had an "agent," but he let it go at that. I didn't push the
issue. Anyways, I met him about a week after Cahir's piece had
been published, and I gave him a copy of both the article and the
book. He was all excited. He was going to have the wife bring

them down to the "agent" she had downtown. He called me two days later. He had a bit of news for me. He said the wife had gone back down that morning to the "agent" again to hand in something, and your boy was inside reading it. He says to her, "This guy's got some fucking voice. Sure we can clean it up here and there, but holy shit!" Did he say anything else? I says to him…."He didn't have to! Congratulations, dude, you have an 'agent.' He'll call you." He was very badly mistaken, though. The man didn't call. I didn't call him either. We somehow managed to hook up on Facebook just. 'Twasn't the end of the matter, though. No, not by a long shot.

Another development shortly after: Eamon, an old friend of mine from twelve-step meetings about the Bronx, gave me a call. He told me both Tony and Dermot above in the Beal Bocht had read the book. The two of them were taken aback by it. They wanted to know if I'd go up and do a reading. I didn't want to, but went up anyway. It went well. I met a lot of old friends up there. I had a good chat with Tony and Dermot as well after. All's I felt leaving the place though was shame. You see as I mentioned above, I was working in the UN. It was a fucking hellhole of a job. We were working our bolloxes off there. Seven days a week, twelve hours a day. Ceilings and walls you couldn't see the end of. Waste of fucking time, though. Uncle Sam was taking the most of it. I was drinking like a cunt. I was as depressed as I'd ever been, and I was completely isolated in the head. It was torture getting up hungover going to that job every morning. For a whole year I did it. I was dead on the inside, but may as well of been dead full stop. Writing was out of the question, and 'twas killing me. The despair that came along with it was brutal. Every day I wanted to open the laptop. I'd make an attempt here and there, but an indescribable fear would come about whenever I did. I'd just sit there frozen with fear, not knowing what the fuck it was I was so afraid of. So who the fuck did I think I was, going up there to do a reading? I felt like a complete fraud. I'd lost total interest in the book as well at the time. I did another reading in Arlene's Grocery shortly after, and let it go at that. I said to myself, I'm an alcoholic plasterer, and I'd better just fucking well remember it.

The job ended six months later. Vivian and Sylvie went down to Phoenix to see the grandmother. I had no interest in looking for work. I had a shitload of money though, and a lot of free time. I went on a weeklong bender that ended up as usual in the back of an ambulance. I did a hellish seven-day detox then of Xanax and booze inside in Beth Israel. I came out and started going to meetings again. I ran inta Eamon from the Bronx at one over in the West Village. I dunno how the topic came up, but we talked a bit about the feasibility of writing a screenplay for the book. You see, anyone who'd ever read it had said to me it'd be a killer screenplay. I wouldn't know how to go about writing it, though, so I'd need a bit of help with it. He suggested an old friend from Belfast. I hesitated on account of not having talked to him for fourteen years. We'd had some kinda falling out you see in a men's psychodrama group. To this day I don't know what it was about. Neither does he. Long story short, Eamon persuaded me to call the "Belfastman," which I did. He read the book and said it could be done. We met up in Spain and had another weeklong psychodrama there. That's another story, though. He told me I'd need to get the book out there more, to drive up a bit of interest in the film. I asked him what would "getting it out there a bit more" look like?' He says to me off the top of his head, ten thousand copies. How the fuck am I supposed to do that? I wouldn't be fit to sell water to a half-dead tourist lost in a desert. I came back to New York invigorated, though. I started to do a bit of writing again. I decided to take some time off work on account of having gotten a job with the city. I'd be on probation for a year, so I wouldn't be able to take any time off till it was over. I put a bit of thought inta pushing the book out and got a bit creative. A couple of very good reviews came in. I advertised it a bit, copies started to go out, but ten thousand was going to take some doing. Then I came across KDP Direct on Amazon. A subsidiary of theirs had published the book for me, and as a result of that I was eligible to enroll in the program. All it basically does is that for five days, you can list the Kindle version for free. I thought it made sense. It did. A few thousand units started flying out fairly rapidly. Amazon has another subsidiary that watches what is selling and reports it on a weekly basis. On the third day of the promotion, they tweeted the week's best sellers: *Butcher a Hog* was number one in memoirs in the free-sales section. No fucking money, but it was getting out there.

Then another development—the tweet automatically went to my Facebook page. The next day I got a message from the "agent" downtown that I'd hooked up with on "FB" simply saying that he'd read that book. We went back and forth a bit, and a week later I went inta meet him. We sat and talked for a coupla hours. A week later I signed a contract. We were in business. No guarantees, but I have a lot of faith in the man.

I started the job with the city. I thought it'd be a cushy number, and I'd be able to get a bit of writing done. I was very badly mistaken on the first thought, but not the second. It's been nothing but a fucking nightmare since. Politics, cockroaches, and the lazy bastards abound. They start going on about their pensions then and how long more they have left in, and it sickens me. I'll hafta stay for fifteen to get it. Fuck that, if I thought I'd still be here in a year I'd put a gun to my head and have done with it. Why I was right about the second thought is on account of what better motivation does a man have to write? Yeah, maybe at some point it'd enable me to get outta this shithole. I started getting up an hour earlier than I hafta every morning and having a go at the typing. I already have the second novel well down the road I do.

'Twas tough going at first getting used to the roaches, but I'm fairly well desensitized to the little bastards at this stage I am. I must've about a hundred thousand of them plastered inta walls by now. And anyhow the roaches are the least of it. I was working with an old Irish boy this day, and the place was crawling with them. I was bitching and moaning on account of them crawling up the inside of the trouser leg near enough far up as the balls. The old boy took note of my distress. He turns around and says to me "Kid, you better get used of it, because I'm telling you—you ain't seen nothing yet!" I found out what he meant that very next morning. I hadta have a toilet disconnected to plaster the wall in behind it. It was left sitting in the hallway. There was an old Spanish boy drunk as a stick inside in the apartment. I mixed a gauge and went at it. Ten minutes later, I started gagging and retching on account of an indescribable foul odor. I took the T-shirt off me and tied it around the face. I chanced it and peeked my head out the door to see where it was coming from. I didn't have far to look. No, there my boy was sitting on the disconnected toilet taking a shit inta it.

Since said incident I've been getting up two hours earlier than need be. The writing has also intensified dramatically.

"When anyone asks me about the Irish character, I say look at the trees. Maimed, stark, and misshapen, but ferociously tenacious."

## Edna O'Brien

*(Born December 15, 1930)*

# Mary Pat Kelly

Mary Pat Kelly was born and raised in Chicago. She worked in Hollywood as a screenwriter for Paramount and Columbia Pictures and in New York City as an associate producer with *Good Morning America* (1976) and *Saturday Night Live* (1980–82). In 1978 she wrote *Martin Scorsese: The First Decade* and in 1997 published a novel, *Special Intentions*, based on her experiences as a nun on the West Side of Chicago. She received her Ph.D. from the City University of New York Graduate Center and has taught at City College and LaGuardia Community College. Her best-selling novel *Galway Bay* was published in 2009. She followed it in 2015 with *Of Irish Blood*. She lives in Manhattan with her husband, Martin Sheerin.

# Finding New York, New York

I watched Martin Scorsese's first movie fifty years ago in the basement of the convent where I was studying to be a nun. Now I'm with my husband at the premiere of *Silence*, Martin Scorsese's latest picture, reclining in one of the oversized stadium-style seats in front of a giant screen in the Regal Theater on Forty-second Street, waiting for the story of seventeenth-century Jesuit martyrs in Japan to begin. Remembering. To use Scorsese's father's storytelling intro, I'm going back a lot of years to Providence Convent, on the campus of Saint Mary-of-the-Woods College, near Terre Haute, Indiana. I'm in my fourth year of sister formation, a junior at the college preparing to teach high school English and drama. Martin Scorsese has sent me his student film *It's Not Just You Murray* in response to a letter that I wrote to New York University but that my teacher Sister Marie Denise had to mail for me. See, it's 1965, and while soon things will change for nuns, now sisters in formation like me can only correspond with family members in once-a-week letters that are turned in to our Superior to be read, stamped, and sent out. Those are the rules. But I have two allies among the college teachers: Sister Marie Denise Sullivan, head of the English Department, and Sister Mary Olive O'Connell, who presides in legendary fashion over the Drama Department. It was in her wonderfully cluttered anti-institutional office/greenroom that I found under a pile of magazines a reprint of a *Harper's* article titled "Students Who Make Movies," about the new phenomenon of film schools and the young director Martin Scorsese, whose student film, described as "a comic satire," won the 1964 Producers' Guild Award. *Mmmm.*

I loved movies. Missed movies. I wanted to see this movie. Maybe I could even use it as the basis for the senior thesis

252

required for English majors. I could discuss the way a director tells a story using images compared to an author's use of words. And now I'm managing to thread Scorsese's film through the old 16mm projector Sister Marie Denise has smuggled out of the Biology Department. As soon as the title character, Murray, appears on the basement wall, Sister Marie Denise and I know. Here is talent, genius even. Scorsese's movie is funny, original, touching, with allusions to everyone from Busby Berkeley to Fellini and featuring his mother in an important role. The central character reminds me of the businessmen in *Grace,* the story James Joyce wrote when he was about the same age as the young director. In both works, men rationalize their lives, deluding themselves about reality, yet their creators reveal the essence of these men to the audience.

Here was James Joyce's epiphany theory in action—the parts of an object are arranged so that we see beyond the "vestment of its appearance," and "the soul of the commonest object" becomes radiant. "The object achieves its epiphany." While Joyce uses words, Scorsese uses camera movements and editing techniques. But both young men had grown up believing that such transformations were possible. After all, didn't the ordinary objects of bread and wine through the mystery of transubstantiation become the body and blood of Christ? The appearance might remain the same, but the essence was changed. Now, that's a tough thing to wrap your mind around at age seven, but every Catholic child who processes up to their First Communion has some notion of that doctrine. I wondered how that belief influenced artists like Scorsese and Joyce. Sister Marie Denise approved my topic.

I wrote another letter, this time directly to Scorsese, and got permission to send it myself—and a stamp. After all, now I was working on an academic project. So began the correspondence that would one day bring me to New York and lead me to explore my Irish-American experience through my own books and films. I smile when I think of those letters. He would send sixteen, seventeen pages typed with such emphasis that the periods went through the onionskin paper, full of his enthusiasm for movies, information about the elements of film-making, and suggestions for books that I should read.

You wouldn't imagine an Italian-American from Elizabeth Street on the Lower East Side, a student and then a teacher at NYU, would have much in common with an Irish-American girl from Chicago on her way to becoming a nun. But Scorsese told me in his very first letter that he too thought he'd had a vocation. At age ten, he'd wanted to become a Maryknoll missionary, but then a newly ordained priest, Father Francis Principe, came to his parish, Saint Patrick's Old Cathedral, with exciting new ideas about theology, literature, music, politics, and the movies. Scorsese and I had both grown up where the parish was the center of our lives. We'd immersed ourselves in rituals both mysterious and familiar. And while the nuns who taught us were "other," they still somehow belonged to us. Then in 1960, being a Catholic got much more exciting. John Fitzgerald Kennedy was elected president and John XXIII became pope. Vatican II opened the windows of the church. The gospel of social justice was embodied for Scorsese at the Catholic worker's house on his own block. Young Catholics like us were going to follow the radical principles of Jesus and change the world.

So as a freshman in high school, he entered New York's Diocesan Preparatory Seminary intending to be a priest like Father Principe. And though he stayed for only one year, the decision and the time spent there marked him.

"My whole life has been religion and the movies. That's it, nothing else," he'd tell me in the 1990 book I wrote, *Martin Scorsese: A Journey*, a follow-up to *Martin Scorsese: The First Decade*, which I wrote in 1978. When I interviewed Father

Principe and told him how much I appreciated Scorsese's response to my letters, he wasn't surprised. "Marty always was kind."

In the letters, we discussed movies and religion. Scorsese was pleased when I wrote that our elderly nun librarian had ordered the books that he had recommended from the Gotham Book Mart, though I had to explain there was no chance I'd be able to see *Hiroshima Mon Amour,* as I had to ask permission even to walk outside in the Grove.

The next year, I went on my first assignment teaching at Providence High School on Chicago's West Side, where Dr. Martin Luther King lived during his campaign against racism in the north. Our nuns had marched with him in Selma, and nearby parishes had supported his effort. I was out of the cloister and into the struggle. Hurray!

That same fall of 1967, Scorsese's first feature was being shown as part of the Chicago Film Festival at the Playboy Theater. My Superior, Sister Marcella O'Malley, said I could go. I watched *I Call First,* which would become *Who's That Knocking at My Door,* in full habit. But I was not as out of place as you'd think, because the movie was infused with a Catholicism that played out against a rock 'n' roll soundtrack. Scorsese's main character, J.R., in his early twenties, lives with his parents in a Little Italy apartment where a picture of the Sacred Heart and a crucifix hang on the wall and a statue of Our Lady sits on the dresser. He meets a girl from outside the neighborhood—with her own place full of books and without a TV. They fall in love. But when she tells him she has been raped on a date, J.R. is stunned. She's not a virgin, not a "good girl." Though he tries to empathize, he's caught in a moral code that views her as damaged, a fallen woman. They break up. J.R. goes back to hang out with the guys within the tribe once more.

Though I came from a background very different from J.R.'s,

I understood the conflict between the Catholic morality we'd absorbed growing up and a world that was changing. In fact, as I watched the movie, I wondered if I hadn't been motivated in part to join the convent as a way of avoiding temptation and staying a "good girl" forever. In less than a year, I too had to decide whether or not to obey the old rules.

The majority of girls I taught at Providence High School were African-American. We read *The Autobiography of Malcolm X* and, as the kids said, put some soul into the spring musical, *Annie Get Your Gun*. And then Dr. Martin Luther King was murdered. During the memorial Mass in the auditorium, just as the school choir was singing "Dream the Impossible Dream," the neighborhood around us erupted. Madison Street was on fire. Reports of looting. A night of chaos. The National Guard drove tanks into Garfield Park and for days the neighborhood was shut off from the rest of the city. Everything was closed. Sister Marcella opened the school to our neighbors, sharing food from the convent pantry. And on Palm Sunday, I joined a group of marchers who were handing out palms to unamused guardsmen on Jackson Boulevard near Our Lady of Sorrows church.

The order was not pleased with me. I was to be transferred to a boarding school in the suburbs of another city. Then Bobby Kennedy was assassinated. A call went out to fulfill his mission by protesting the Vietnam War and aiding those living in poverty. I could not remain inside the convent. I left and joined the Poor People's Campaign in Washington, sponsored by the Southern Christian Leadership Conference founded by Dr. King. I spent most of the summer of 1968 in the SCLC encampment, Resurrection City, on the Washington Mall, until we were driven out by tear gas. The campaign moved to Chicago, where we demonstrated on Michigan Avenue during the Democratic party's convention, and where I was teargassed again.

I found a job with an anti-poverty program on the West Side of Chicago in the neighborhood where I had taught, and worked there for a year. But with Nixon as president, the war on poverty became bureaucratic and ineffective. I felt I was a cog in an unjust system. Like so many of my generation, I hit the road and spent six months traveling in Europe.

My parents and siblings had moved to New York, where I'd lived twice before, once in grade school and before that during World War II. My father was a Navy pilot flying escort duty for the Atlantic convoys out of Floyd Bennett Field, and my mother and newly born me had an apartment on Ocean Parkway in Brooklyn. Growing up in Chicago, I'd bragged about that early Brooklyn connection. So when I returned from Europe to spend Easter in New York with my family, I contacted Martin Scorsese. We spoke for the first time. "Let's go to the movies," he said.

*Popi*, with Alan Arkin, was playing at the Waverley Theater in Greenwich Village, and he thought I should see it. We met in front of the theater. He looked exactly like his picture in *Harper's* magazine, though now his hair was shoulder-length. He wore jeans and a very white oxford-cloth shirt. Both well pressed. He told me that after four years of stop-and-go production and a long search for a distributor, *Who's That Knocking at My Door* had finally come to theaters in September 1969, "announcing," as critic Roger Ebert said, "the arrival of an important director." A good start, but Scorsese was trying to make more movies, and supported himself by teaching at NYU.

After the movie, we went to an Italian coffeehouse for espresso. Scorsese was as intense in person as he was on paper. He'd gone to the Woodstock music festival to work as an assistant director and an editor on the documentary *Woodstock,* scheduled to open the next week.

"We were going to a music festival, so I brought a dress

shirt and cuff links," he said, and laughed. He'd been in Paris during the May '68 student uprisings. We talked about the Vietnam War and ways to stop it. I told him about the protest I had joined in Washington and in Chicago and my work in the anti-poverty program. He told me he'd made an anti-war short, *The Big Shave*, that had won a prize, and he was writing a script that would expand on the characters and stories in *Who's That Knocking*, titled *Season of the Witch*. It would become *Mean Streets*.

"But my professor, Haig Manoogian, who also was the producer of *Who's That Knocking*, told me not to do any more pictures about Italians." We laughed. I thought of the courage Scorsese showed in putting his own experiences up on the screen. Later, Pauline Kael would call *Mean Streets* a "triumph of personal filmmaking," but that evening "personal filmmaking" meant taking a risk. Hollywood movies weren't made about neighborhood guys or Catholicism as lived from the inside.

Scorsese asked me if I was still interested in movies. Well, yes, I said, but my life had none of the drama of his coming of age. Dutch elms arched over the streets in my neighborhood and, as Frank McCourt would later write, "a happy childhood is hardly worth your while." I told Scorsese how much I admired his bred-in-the-bone understanding of Italian America. He told me that he had known his grandfather, who had come from Sicily, and that there were people on Elizabeth Street, where he grew up, who only spoke Italian, or one of the dialects of southern Italy. A local movie theater showed Italian-language films, and opera played from many windows.

I said that all I knew about the background of my family was that the Kellys had been in Chicago a long time. And while we were very proud that our roots were in Ireland, I had no real information about where we were from. Our context was

America, Chicago. The Irish songs we sang were "Cheer Cheer for Old Notre Dame," and "McNamara's Band." We believed that the "Fighting Irish" would win overall and that we were "the finest in the land." John F. Kennedy and Grace Kelly embodied our victory.

It was my students at Providence High School who had important stories to tell. Now, in the letters Scorsese and I had exchanged, I'd mentioned that I had written for the college magazine.

I explained that Ireland was a land of myth and magic. In fact, I hadn't even planned to go there on my European trip. It would have been like setting out for Brigadoon, I said.

My friend, also Irish-American, and I had started our travels in London and had arranged to rent a room in a house by phone. When we arrived, the woman who opened the door said to us, "Oh, girls, I'm such a silly billy—I forgot to ask your names." When my friend said she was Ann O'Neill and I told her that my name was Mary Pat Kelly, she said to us, "You're Irish." I told Scorsese we thought she was complimenting us; instead, she slammed the door in our faces.

Scorsese found that very interesting and asked how I'd reacted. I told him that I hadn't really understood what had happened until I met an African student at a Howlin' Wolf concert who said that the English were still prejudiced against the Irish. He told me that in London I was black like him. Naturally, I said to Scorsese, we went to Ireland.

He asked me what my impressions had been, and then I just started talking. Faster and faster. The people, the landscape, the stories, the history I'd known so little about, and some of the things I'd learned regarding the civil-rights struggles happening in Northern Ireland.

"I'd say you found your subject," he said. "Haig Manoogian is teaching a course called Sight and Sound this summer at NYU,"

Scorsese told me. "You should enroll." And he even offered me a job. He was programming films for a summer-long festival called Movies in the Park and needed an assistant. So there it was, my chance. I even had a place to live. As I said, my four sisters, brother, and parents were here in the city, as my father's advertising career had brought him to New York. But I'd left the convent to work on Chicago's West Side. I was already feeling guilty about taking my European break. Plus, young women in 1970 were teachers, social workers, nurses, secretaries—not, gulp, artists. I went back to Chicago. I enquired and found that I could probably get my old job back.

My landlady, Samella Williams, had sublet my apartment, but the tenant had left and I was back on the second floor of her two-flat wondering what to do. I spent every evening that last week in April sitting on the porch with her and our neighbors drinking beer. Good talk. Lots of laughs. Except one night Mrs. Williams said to me, "You're too young to be sitting on the porch watching the world go by. You'd better put your hat on backwards and start stepping." But stepping where?

The next day, National Guardsmen killed four students who were protesting the Vietnam War on the Kent State campus in Ohio. I remembered the song we would sing at Resurrection City, "Which side are you on? Which side are you on?" Mrs. Williams was right—I had to choose a side. I couldn't go back to life as usual, but New York still seemed a gamble.

Two nights later, I was alone watching the final of the New York Knicks–Celtic series. Now, this was long before our Chicago Bulls made us winners. We were used to losing, and the hereditary enemy was New York. Just before the game started, the announcer said that the Knicks' center, Willis Reed, had injured his ankle and would not play. At first I thought, Good, let the Knicks lose. But then Reed limped onto the court and made two quick baskets. Alone in my apartment, I cheered along with the crowd on TV. And felt a kind of hope. Somehow Willis Reed's action was a sign that Kent State wasn't our destiny. The good guys were going to win. The Vietnam War would one day be over and we were marching toward racial justice. A moment of grace.

An epiphany.

Scorsese created such out-of-time spaces in his movies, and suddenly I very much wanted to try to do the same. I put my hat on backwards and moved to New York.

So now, fifty years later, the lights are going down and here I am in this Forty-second Street theater, a New York resident who has lived in the same apartment on the Upper West Side since 1970. In the beginning, I'd taken jobs like doing surveys for the Gallup Poll or selling girdles in the Plymouth shop on Broadway to survive. I very much valued the years I spent teaching in the City University of New York system while getting my Ph.D. at the Graduate Center. But in the last twenty-five years, I had somehow managed to earn a living as a writer and filmmaker, telling Irish and Irish-American stories.

The first images of *Silence* appear. Wow! Here it is. All of Scorsese's mastery plus everything he's discovered during his own spiritual journey up there on the screen like no movie I'd ever seen before. *America* magazine would call the picture "a masterpiece." And these are the Jesuits speaking. Who would know better how to judge this tale of Jesuits in seventeenth-century Japan? Some of the priests chose martyrdom; others became apostates for reasons that seemed moral at the time.

As I watch, I think of the priests beheaded in Ireland under the Penal Laws and of the tens of thousands of Irish people, most of them nameless, tortured just as brutally as the Japanese were for refusing to give up the faith. Though I don't think Oliver Cromwell gave them a choice.

I picture the Mass Rocks still in caves in Galway and Donegal, the places where our ancestors gathered secretly, risking their lives to receive Communion from a priest just as the Japanese Christians do in *Silence*. I thought too of the story I had told of my own great-great-grandmother in Galway Bay and the courage that kept millions from trading their Catholicism for a bowl of soup when conversion to Protestantism became the price for being fed during Ireland's Great Starvation.

This Irish connection was strengthened by the fact that Liam Neeson was playing the Portuguese Jesuit central character, Father Ferreira, and Ciarán Hinds his Italian Superior Father Valignano. But the movie was also reminding me of a more recent, more personal experience.

What?

Oh, right. I'd spent the last two weeks of the presidential campaign canvasing for Hillary Clinton in Bucks County, Pennsylvania. One afternoon I went from door to door in a neighborhood where the lawns were overrun with Trump signs. Some of the placards were printed by the Republican party with the slogan "Hillary for Prison." I had a list of registered Democrats and knocked on one door. A woman about my age came out onto the stoop, but as we talked, she looked around at the Trump displays in front of the neighboring houses and lowered her voice until we were almost whispering. A man came out of his house and shook his fist at us. She stepped quickly in. Later, back at the house serving as our headquarters, I said I felt like a Christian in the catacombs. The scene came back to me as I watched *Silence*.

Now, I'm not going to push this analogy too far, but during the canvas I did have a sense of being under siege in unfriendly territory. It made me want to connect with those who shared my faith. I knew the need to cluster with other like-minded people to strengthen my wobbly knees. In the same way

Scorsese helped me become an artist fifty years ago, *Silence* was compelling me to honesty, self-examination, guts, in the face of our disastrous election. I had used a quote from Isaiah to begin *Martin Scorsese: A Journey*—"the burning sands will become pools and the thirsty ground springs of water. A highway will be there called the Holy Way. No fool shall go astray on it. No lion will be there. It is for those with a journey to make."

In his interview with the editor of *America*, Jim Martin, S.J., Scorsese had said of his own spiritual journey, "It's a pilgrimage. We're on the road." Yes, I thought, back on the road again.

"Read everything. Write all the time. And if you can do anything else that gives you equal pleasure and allows you to sleep soundly at night, do that instead. The writing life is an odd one to say the least."

## *Alice McDermott*
*(Born June 27, 1953)*

# Colin Broderick

Colin Broderick emigrated from County Tyrone in 1988. He studied poetry at Lehman College with Billy Collins. In 2009 he published his first memoir, *Orangutan*. His second, *That's That*, was published in 2014. He made a short movie, *Smile*, in 2015. In 2016 he wrote and directed a feature movie, *Emerald City*, loosely based on his life as a construction worker in New York City trying to formulate a life as a writer. He lives in Woodstock, New York, with his wife and two kids, Samuel and Erica.

# Lucky

The New York I arrived in twenty-eight years ago was one of abandoned buildings, battered window shades, and blackened shells along the highway. Uptown was boom-box, squeegee men, and sneaker wars. Down on the Deuce they were shilling sleaze and switchblades for as cheap as a buck. Pickpockets, peddlers, and preachers stood shoulder to shoulder with ruddy-faced Irish-American cops too outnumbered and sweaty to give a goddamn. Back then, Forty-second Street was a scabbed vein, so pockmarked and contaminated it was practically its own ecosystem.

Downtown was squatters' rights, artists, and dope dealers alongside old-school Eastern European grandmothers in headscarves lugging shopping bags up Second Avenue. Street walkers bold as peacocks preened themselves on the cobblestoned streets of the West Village while over around Saint Mark's, pale-faced boys in skinny pants and Mohawks graffitied shuttered tenement walls and nodded out in Tompkins Square Park. New York was a city of shadows and ghosts and blocks you didn't dare venture down alone.

It was a town that felt lived in. A town with an active working class. A man could be a carpenter and still manage to raise a family in a two-bedroom apartment on the Upper East Side. An artist could still afford to live in a cavernous, paint-spattered loft in TriBeCa without sacrificing his creative spirit to a management company. Madness and danger were a staple of everyday life. Not that it was easy; it was a hustle. It was a dodge and a weave, blindfolded and drunk through a minefield. Each new step possibly your last. But man, was it alive; an urban landscape so rich in story that words practically rained down off the fire escapes like rust chips and danced their way into my soul in ready-made paragraphs.

Being young and Irish in New York, I was bequeathed the added romance of a literary heritage, even if I didn't understand it fully back then. There was a certain expectation in being Irish and being a writer. It was never going to be enough just to be average in this town. As an Irish writer in New York, it was my duty to shoulder the past like a gilded coffin. New York is where Irish literature comes to get its passport stamped. Fail to pass muster and they'll send you packing; succeed and they'll grudgingly endure your presence.

As a young writer with a silent pledge to the pen in my heart, I would stand in bookstores all over town, dreaming. One day I would write something good enough to sit here. One day I would see my name on the spine of a book, on a shelf, wedged next to Banville and Behan. I believed that when that day arrived, I would feel complete. I would have honored my life's destiny. I would be happy.

There was only one small catch: I couldn't write.

I could drink, though. Boy, could I drink! And when I drank, I could see myself up there at the podium, the crowd applauding my words. So I drank some more. I drank my way through dive bar after dive bar. Drank myself into trouble all over town. Drank myself all the way to the West Coast, where I bought an old Buick and a dark pair of shades. I was Jim Morrison. I was Kerouac, Bukowski, and Baudelaire all rolled into one. When I woke from the dream, the phone was ringing. It was my mother. She was panicked and scared, telling me that my father wanted to get on a plane to San Francisco that very morning to take me home. "Don't you remember calling last night? You were crying. You were saying you were lost." I was lost.

Shortly after that I got sober, for the first time. I came back to New York, moved into an apartment in the Bronx, and began my first real scribblings, hitting open-mike readings all over town for inspiration.

Poetry was big in New York in the nineties. I saw some of the greatest poets of our time perform in small smoky rooms: Allen Ginsberg, Alice Walker, Stanley Kunitz, John Ashberry, Sharon Olds, Charles Simic, Paul Muldoon, to name just a few. I was a good listener; I listened with my heart. I was receiving an education, and these voices were the source, the deep well of experience where I would dip my cup.

I sat my SATs and enrolled at Lehman College to study with a young up-and-coming poet whose work I really admired, Billy Collins. I opened a used bookstore/coffeeshop of my own and held weekly readings there for a time. I was writing a little but I was still too nervous to expose my work to the world. Without alcohol, I was not as brave as I had imagined myself to be, and writing, much to my surprise, was hard work.

But I was writing. I was getting into the work of being a writer. I wrote novels, plays, and short stories. At twenty-six, I sent my first novel, *Church End*, out into the world—and never heard from it again. I wrote another, *The Blue Store*, about an Irish boy named Elvis in search of his father. I sent it out too. I was sure this would be the one. But the mailman kept my letterbox hungry and thin with circulars and utility bills.

I read a novel called *Songdogs* by a young Irish writer named Colum McCann. It had magic in it. Even its title had a rare knock-kneed poetry to it. McCann wasn't much older than me. I found out he was reading downtown at Barnes & Noble on Union Square. I waited online while he signed copies of his new book, *This Side of Brightness*. When I reached him, I nervously handed him my manuscript and asked him if he'd be so kind as to read it and tell me what he thought of it.

"Is it any good?" he asks me.

"I have no idea," I say.

"You want to go to a party?"

There was a launch party for his book that night at Saint Dymphna's on Saint Mark's Place; my first bona fide downtown New York Irish literary event. I felt awkward and out of place. I was too naive at the time to know that was how I was supposed to feel, that events like these are best preserved in snapshots, that the writer's only real solace is at home when the work is going well. But it was an introduction to the public life of the writer: the dog-and-pony show. New York is not interested in Irish writers who toil dutifully in private; there's no copy in it. New York wants its writers unmercifully drunk or half broken by love, wandering the streets mad with poverty or ego. It wants them to say at least one witty thing so it can be carved into an edifice. Who really cared what Brendan Behan or Maeve Brennan wrote when their glorious insanity managed to trump all penmanship in the end!

So after eight years of playing it straight and dutifully logging the hours in my writer's apprenticeship, I got divorced for the second time and went drinking again. Within just a few weeks, I directed my first play, got stabbed, and had my first short story, "Bang," accepted by a literary journal.

One day I got off the train at Seventy-second Street and Broadway. There was a magazine store there at the time on the west side of the avenue that carried all the best literary journals and magazines. I entered the store with the nervous energy of a thief. I scanned the shelves until I saw a copy of *Rattapallax*. I was too nervous to touch it. The gentleman next to me in the tweed jacket reached for it and my heart jumped. Was I was going to witness someone buying my first published story? He hesitated for a moment, his fingers lingering over the issue like the needles of a claw crane, then he dipped gingerly and picked up a copy of *Poetry* magazine instead.

In an act of gluttony I brought the remaining three issues to the counter and bought them all. But once I left the store, I felt horribly sick. Why did I have to take them all? Now there were none left in the store. How was anyone to see my work if I went around buying up all the copies myself? What sort of an egotistical self-centered prick buys his own work? I was tempted to toss the lot into a garbage can on the corner of the block. But I didn't. Instead I boarded the 1 train for the ride back to the Bronx. I needed a good stiff drink. Did I mention I was drinking again? I was thirty-one years old and I was drinking again. I wouldn't write another short story, book, play, or poem for an entire eight years. I drank.

In the summer of 2006 I was thirty-eight years old, living in a fifth-floor walk-up in Hell's Kitchen. The rent went unpaid for months. I was unemployable. I was down to about 115 pounds on a steady diet of beer, vodka, weed, cocaine, and whatever pills I could get my hands on. I had to keep a glass of whiskey next to my bed so that when the shakes and sweats kicked in, after about four hours of unconsciousness, I could reach for it easily to keep the devil's hairy fingers from around my throat. Over the previous eight years of drinking, I had been stabbed, beaten, jailed, and hospitalized. The idea of taking a swan dive off my fifth-floor balcony out onto Ninth Avenue had begun to haunt me as a viable alternative to the chorus of demons that plagued my every waking thought.

One night laying in the dark alone, sipping on whiskey, listening to the blare of traffic below my window, my heart pounding like the drumbeat in some ancient pagan death ritual, I saw that I had reached the very end of the line. I understood that this was the place right before death. If something didn't change soon, they would find me here on the floor of this apartment surrounded by empty bottles. My body would be carted off to the local morgue, family would be notified, they'd ship me home, and bury me in Dunmoyle with my own people.

The landlord would hire a couple of guys to bag the mess I left behind and I would be remembered in the neighborhood as just another unfortunate Irishman who couldn't handle the sauce. I would leave behind no grand literary legacy, no children. In ten years, I'd be all but forgotten, a painful footnote in the family tree. When faced with this void, it was my own unfulfilled potential that stared beseechingly back at me. I knew that it was time to stop drinking and start writing again. Within a week, I'd stopped. I moved to a friend's farmhouse upstate and began work immediately on my first memoir, *Orangutan*.

The problem with alcohol is that it can make you feel like the greatest writer in the world without ever having written a word. The feeling of being great is so powerful that it negates the necessity to write anything at all. For me, alcohol was the medication that kept me hovering above my pain, until one day it didn't.

Once I stopped drinking, I was forced to feel. Writing about my life helped me burrow into the bruised places and heal them by finally articulating the hurt. I'd spent so much of my life romanticizing the myth of the drunk writer that when I finally peeled away the blurry veneer, the truth startled me.

In time I would revisit the writers I adored and examine the consequences of drinking on their lives a little more closely. Hemingway wrote while sober and rewarded himself by drinking heavily in the evenings. At the age of sixty-two, he blew his brains out to end the nightmare of alcoholic paranoia. Four decades later, Hunter S. Thompson practically mirrored his departure. For years I'd managed to romanticize Bukowski as the perfect living example of the drinking man's poet, until I saw a clip of him violently kicking his wife off the end of a couch during a drunken interview. And then there were my Irish forerunners, Fitzgerald, Behan, and Brennan; it turned out they had all done their best writing sober, before the booze destroyed their ability to articulate their art in a coherent manner. Don't get me started on Shane MacGowan. But forget the writing for a moment: what fearful, paranoid lives they endured! Just as I had, fueled by the need to medicate an existential pain born of a series of childhood traumas.

The absence of joy: that is the real heartbreaker for a life half lived. What good is success when your mind is so muddled you can't enjoy a walk in the park with your wife, or you're too paranoid to read your daughter to sleep at night? How horrible never to experience the simple sweetness of curling up with a hot cup of tea and a good book next to a rainy window in November. What good is any measure of external success if the interior life is hell?

I take no glory in the fact that I quit drinking. It was luck, pure and simple. The heartbreaking truth is that most are not so lucky. What I will take ownership for is the work I put into staying sober. I earn my freedom, one day at a time.

Over the last eleven years without a drink, I published two books, directed two of my own plays on the New York stage, published articles and stories in some of the top publications, saw my name in *The New Yorker* and *The New York Times*, took the stage at Lincoln Center to read my own work, wrote and directed my first feature movie. I met my wife, Rachel, and I became a father to a girl and then a boy. I am not rich. I am not a household-name author. But I am still writing. In my own roundabout way, I wound up living the very life that I'd always dreamed might be possible. I am an Irish writer in New York.

# Acknowledgments

There are just a small handful of people I'd like to acknowledge for the time that I worked on this particular book.

First let me thank the angels: Christopher Neill, Frank Bruno, and Ciaran Cassidy for keeping an eye on me as I write.

My parents, Michael and Claire, my brothers and sisters... we're all in this together.

Pam and Jack Murphy. Mike Chibnik.

Thank you to my other family, Tony Caffrey, Josh Brolin, John Duddy, Johnny McConnell.

Con McCormack and Lisa Sullivan: your belief in me gives me strength and faith, thank you.

Cal Kelly, Brendan O'Shea, Patsy Keenan, Dermot Burke, Karl Geary.

The Grat Pack.

Jane Dystel and Miriam Goderich.

Kevin Fortuna and Bill Lavender.

And to the three people who mean more to me than all the books in the world: Rachel, Erica, and Sam... Thank you xxx.

To contact Colin Broderick, or find out more about his books and movies, you can find him at: www.colinbroderick.com

Lavender Ink
lavenderink.org

CPSIA information can be obtained
at www.ICGtesting.com
Printed in the USA
LVHW050537121218
600165LV00023B/2140/P

9 781944 884512